D0952576

ERNIE HARWELL'S
DIAMOND GEMS

ERNIE HARWELL'S
DIAMOND GEMS

Ernie Harwell
Hall-of-Fame Broadcaster

Edited by Geoff Upward

Momentum Books, Ltd.
Ann Arbor, Michigan
1991

COPYRIGHT © 1991 by Ernie Harwell

All rights reserved. No part of this book may be used or reproduced in any manner whatsoever without prior written permission of the publisher, except in the case of brief quotations embodied in critical articles and reviews.

Manufactured in the United States of America

Jacket design by Don Ross

Momentum Books Ltd.
210 Collingwood, Suite 106
Ann Arbor, MI 48103
ISBN 0-9618726-7-5

To two great partners: Lulu Harwell, who has shared her love and her life with me for 50 years; and Paul Carey, who has shared with me his loyalty and consummate professionalism.

Special Thanks to:

Bill Haney, who inspired me to enter into the book-writing business.

Geoff Upward, who corrected my strikeovers, transpositions, bad spelling and other literary sins.

Natasha Monchak, who put it all together with fast and skillful typing.

Chronology: Ernie Harwell

Born Washington, Georgia, January 25, 1918
Atlanta correspondent *The Sporting News,* 1934–1948
Sports department *Atlanta Constitution,* 1936–1940
Sports director WSB Atlanta, 1940–1942
Married Lula Tankersley, August 30, 1941
USMC, 1942–1946
Atlanta Cracker baseball announcer, 1943; 1946–1948
Brooklyn Dodger baseball announcer, 1948–1949
New York Giant baseball announcer, 1950–1953
Baltimore Oriole baseball announcer, 1954–1959
Detroit Tiger baseball announcer, 1960–
Inducted into the Baseball Hall of Fame, August 2, 1981
"Tuned to Baseball" author, 1985

Contents

A Word from the Publisher

"Lo, the winter is past, the rain is over and gone, the flowers appear on the earth, the time of the song of birds is come and the voice of the turtle is heard in our land."

For decades, with those words from the Song of Solomon, Ernie Harwell has greeted Spring and welcomed millions of listeners to the new baseball season.

In the Forties, Ernie was there to call the play-by-play for the Atlanta Crackers and the Brooklyn Dodgers. The Fifties saw him behind the mike for the New York Giants and the Baltimore Orioles. And since 1960, the famous Harwell voice with its whisper of southern pines and sunny days has been beamed far beyond the midwest on the powerful signal of the Detroit Tigers radio network.

So one of the most modest of men became one of the best-known citizens of the midwest and, many would say, one of its best-loved. Among his peers and around the nation, Ernie Harwell stands as one of the most highly regarded announcers in the history of sports play-by-play broadcasting. But because he is so modest, perhaps I should have been prepared for his first response when I asked him in April 1984 to write a book.

"I'm not sure many people would be interested in my little stories," Ernie said. "A lot of them are just long enough to fill a break in the action. I doubt that would make much of a book."

Well, Ernie Harwell was wrong.

As anyone who has ever taken a portable radio to a Detroit Tigers game knows, the words "wrong" and "Ernie Harwell" rarely can be used in the same sentence. When Ernie paints his tableau of the grand old game, his trademarks are precision and accuracy. Ernie breathes life into the game over the radio waves, infuses it with richness, color and excitement, but never at the cost of accuracy. Right away that sets him apart from announcers who get carried away or bored or smitten with creativity and, as a result, present "new and improved" versions of the facts.

An Ernie Harwell account is, first and foremost, dead right on. He will explain, interpret or amplify the action on the field. But he never distorts, never exaggerates. In an Ernie Harwell broadcast—and there have been some eight thousand of them—the game is always the star. What the trusting listener hears in the familiar, mellow voice that has become to so many millions the voice of summer, is exactly what is transpiring on the diamond. The listener knows that Ernie Harwell will be fair. He will be interesting. And he will be right.

But in April 1984, as for whether fans and other readers would be interested in a book of Ernie Harwell stories, Ernie Harwell, for once, was wrong. It didn't take long to prove that. When Ernie's first book, *Tuned to Baseball,* appeared in 1985, fans snapped it up so quickly the presses had to be started again and again and again—seven times in all—to meet demand. There were three reprintings in hardbound. Then four more reprintings in quality paperback. Now, with a national mass market paperback on racks throughout the country, more than one hundred thousand copies are in print of the book that "not many people would be interested in."

But that first book scarcely tapped the vein of baseball lore that is Ernie Harwell.

Ernie has seen countless thousands of stories unfold over the years. He has viewed them from the best seat in baseball at Tiger Stadium and from other catbird seats around the major leagues. And he has seen stories unfold off the fields of play and behind the scenes. He has watched the sustained brilliance of legendary stars and the rapid rise and burnout of one-season phenoms. He has known class acts and charismatic characters. He has watched athletes at their best and at moments they would rather forget. He has studied the diamond game in all its facets. He has been there for the dramatic and the thrilling. He has observed the ridiculous and the comic. He has witnessed moments that are poignant, tender, and heroic. And in his 50 years behind the microphone, he has seen these facets fuse together into the ever-changing but always familiar mosaic of the game.

And it is with his eyes focused on that diamond that this much and rightly honored announcer has discovered some gems. With the careful and skillful touch of Geoff Upward, these gems of America's most American game have been gathered, polished and displayed in these pages.

Enjoy Ernie Harwell's diamond gems. As you turn these pages, you will be viewing a vibrant kaleidoscope of action, events and people through the eyes of one of the most observant, insightful and articulate commentators the game has ever known. And as you read, listen for the sound of that familiar rich baritone—listen to the voice of Ernie Harwell, the sound of sunny summer days at the ballpark.

Bill Haney
February 1991

A Word from the Author

There's always a question about the second time. Maybe it's better to quit while you think you're ahead.

I had that perception just after my broadcasting career had taken me to Baltimore.

In 1954 the Orioles had entered the American League and I was hired as their announcer by National Beer. I had been on the job only a few days when Norm Almony, vice president in charge of National's marketing, phoned me.

"Ernie," he said, "tonight I'm entertaining a group of our top salesmen at the Oasis. Come over for a short while and meet them."

The Oasis was one of the several upholstered sewers on the infamous Baltimore Block. It was a smoky dive which featured undressed ladies and a notorious pasty-faced emcee named Sid Gray. Dutifully, I reported to the Oasis and mingled with the National Beer salesmen. We were seated around minuscule tables surrounded by well-endowed, over-ripe strippers, struggling toward exotica.

Suddenly Sid Gray grabbed the microphone. "Ladies

and gentlemen," he shouted, "let me introduce our great Oriole announcer, a man doing a fantastic job." (I'd only been in Baltimore a few days and I'm sure that neither Sid nor many of the others had heard me broadcast.) "We love him. He is terrific. Let's have a big hand for Ernie Harwell."

Reluctantly, I rose and waved at the crowd, which was as enthusiastic about me as a motorist being served a speeding citation. I sat down as soon as I could.

Then, to my dismay, Gray had grabbed the mike and was introducing me again.

"He's great, folks. He's great. Ernie, stand up again and take another bow."

Again, I rose to my feet. As I was standing, Gray flashed a toothless grin and shouted, "Sit down, you sonovabitch. Nobody wants to look at you."

That's what I mean about the second time.

Nevertheless, after my first book, *Tuned To Baseball,* I'm trying again. I only hope you won't put *Diamond Gems* down as abruptly as emcee Sid Gray put me down that night at the Oasis.

E. H.
February 1991

Introduction

Not long ago I was reading a Bennett Cerf book that had a small section on baseball humor. Most of the stories rehashed the old, moldy tales which I'm sure many of you have read.

But the stories did bring a couple of thoughts to me.

The anecdotes of baseball seem to be repeated for each generation of fans with a different set of characters. Many times I've seen a story run the gamut. In the early 1900s the story would be about Germany Schaefer or Rube Waddell. In another ten years, the name would change to Bugs Raymond, then to Dizzy Dean, Jim Piersall or Yogi Berra. In fact, there's one story told about Berra which I traced to pre-Civil War days. Back then, the locale was a courtroom instead of a baseball field.

It goes this way:

Yogi Berra turns on an umpire and disputes his call at the plate.

"You'd better get back there and catch," the umpire tells him, "or I'll bite your head off."

"If you do," answers Yogi, "you'll have more brains in your stomach than you've got in your head."

This story was attributed to Alexander Stephens, one-time vice president of the Confederate States of America. He used the put-down while a Georgia Congressman, long before the Civil War. And, I might guess that the retort could be traced to an even earlier time.

Another point about baseball stories—most of the so-called funny ones didn't happen on the field. They were dialogs between players, or a player and an umpire, or a player and a manager. Most could just have easily been about an event in a factory, office or school.

I can recall one well-known incident from the field. The story doesn't seem too funny in print, but it would have been a whopper to witness. While managing the Brooklyn Dodgers, Casey Stengel came out to protest an umpire's decision. Before he reached the plate, he doffed his cap and out flew a sparrow. That one has been repeated often. Still, I'd like to have been there.

Another old chestnut is the spring training story about another Dodger manager, Wilbert Robinson. Casey is in this one, too. Robby has bragged that he can catch a baseball dropped from an airplane. The bets are made and a crowd gathers.

Up in the plane with the pilot, Stengel crouches. But instead of a baseball, he drops a grapefruit. Robby circles under it and just manages to get his big mitt on it. The grapefruit splatters all over him. He thinks he's dying and covered with blood. It was a harmless, but funny, practical joke.

Nearly twenty years ago, I was fortunate enough to see a funny one myself. Yet, the crowd, including me, didn't realize the humor of the situation at the time.

The date was July 15, 1973, and the Tigers were playing California. On May 15, Nolan Ryan had pitched a no-hitter in Kansas City. Now the Angel fireballer was pitching another one against the Tigers. I have never seen a pitcher more devastating than Ryan was that Sunday afternoon in Detroit. Not only was he fast, he was also throwing a great curve, which made his blinding speed that much more effective. Ryan was so overwhelming that it was an event when a Tiger could even foul off a pitch.

The game was hitless when Tiger first baseman Norman Cash came to the plate in the sixth. Norm was frustrated. He already had fanned twice in his two trips. But before he could step into the batter's box, umpire Ron Luciano called "Time." He sent Norm to the dugout to get another bat.

Cash's bat was illegal. That's all we knew at the time. None of us realized that despite the game's tension, Mr. Cash still had his sense of humor. The illegal "bat" was not a bat at all. It was a table leg—the leg off an old battered table in the Tiger clubhouse.

It didn't work: Luciano saw to that. The table leg was soon back in the bat rack, and, with his legal bat, Norm bounced to second. And Ryan went on to achieve his second no-hitter of the year. But you can't say Norm didn't try. And you can't say he let the drama of the moment stifle his sense of humor.

I doubt if Cash's performance will ever make any anthology of humor. But I'll always remember Norm as the man who tried to break up a no-hitter with a table leg.

This is one of baseball's anecdotal "gems" for me—a story about a truly colorful character. I have heard and retold many such stories over my 50-year baseball broadcasting career to listening audiences in Atlanta, New York, Baltimore and Detroit. Some I've seen, some have been told to me by the players or managers involved, others are apocryphal, others still simply legend. Whatever the source, they're part of baseball and I love 'em. I hope you do too.

ONE

With a Little Help from My Friends

"The small boy does not know that the best third baseman in baseball is human; that he fights with his wife,
worries about bills and occasionally swears at the bat
boy. All the small boy knows is that the third baseman
is his hero, and a hero always does the right thing."

Robert W. Creamer

His name was Orenthal and he lived in the slums
of San Francisco. By the time he was 13, Orenthal
was a member of a gang, the Persian Warriors.
Each year the gang held a dance and they needed liquor.
So, they devised a way to get it.

Four or five of the Warriors would go to a liquor store
and two of them would stage a fight. While the owner
tried to separate the fighters, the others would stuff whis-
key bottles into their jackets, then they would all run.

In 1961, Orenthal was on the refreshment committee.
That meant he had to hit a few stores. Unfortunately,
he picked one where the owners recognized him. When

he got home from the dance that night, the police were waiting and they locked him up.

Orenthal's mom and dad were separated, and when he needed discipline his dad came home to deliver it. He dreaded facing his father. His mother picked him up at the juvenile home and brought him home. He waited in his room for the inevitable beating from his dad. Soon, he dozed off.

When he woke, he heard voices downstairs in the living room. He went down the steps. To his amazement, there stood Willie Mays, his hero. He had no idea why Willie Mays was there ... it seemed like a miracle.

Mays was at his peak then. He *was* the Giants. People were always talking about Willie. Orenthal had gone to his first game, at Candlestick Park, when he was 10 years old. His Uncle Hollis took him, and Orenthal couldn't take his eyes off Willie Mays. Mays even hit a home run that afternoon. Orenthal began to imitate Willie. He was his hero—almost a god to him.

And here was Willie Mays in Orenthal's living room. Why?

Uncle Hollis, it seems, had spoken to a man named Lefty Gordon, who was a youth counselor. Gordon had contacted Mays and told him about this fine young athlete who was on the verge of getting into deep trouble.

So, Willie Mays came to help. And he helped in his own way —no lecture, no teaching. He simply asked Orenthal to spend the afternoon with him. He went to the dry cleaners, then to a store to buy something. They went to the house of a friend of Mays where a banquet was being planned. And Willie took Orenthal to his San Francisco home.

After three hours, Willie took Orenthal back to his home. To the relief of Orenthal, his dad was not there. In fact, his father never again whipped him.

Mays made Orenthal realize a dream. He helped him turn his life around. Orenthal knew that Willie Mays, his hero, was a real person, a true human being, and that there was a chance for him.

It was the pivotal afternoon in Orenthal's life ... and he has never forgotten it.

The story could have a terrific climax if I told you that young Orenthal, the super teenage athlete, grew up to play center field for the Giants. But that wouldn't be true.

No, but he did excel in another sport—the sport of football. Orenthal's full name: Orenthal James "O. J." Simpson.

Don't try to sock me with the generalized condemnation that big-league baseball players are all insensitive louts. I know better. Let me give you a personal experience that I will never forget.

My late father-in-law, A. N. "Pete" Peters was a great fan of the Cincinnati Reds, especially Johnny Bench. Several springs ago, when the Reds were scheduled to play the Detroit Tigers at Lakeland, I took a tape recorder so I could ask Johnny Bench to tape a message to Pete.

Well, that afternoon Bench was injured and stayed back in Tampa. However, Marty Brennaman, the Reds' announcer, came to the rescue. He took my cassette and told me he'd have Bench tape a message for Mr. Peters.

Sure enough, by the next week Pete had his own message from Johnny Bench and a bonus—one from Brennaman, too.

"Hi, Pete, this is Johnny Bench," the tape said. "Hear you haven't been feeling too well lately. Well, get well soon 'cause we want you to keep on rooting for our Reds."

I have never seen a thrill or a happiness like that reflected in Pete's face when he heard that tape.

That was mid-March. In less than two months Pete had died. But before he died, he kept playing that taped message from Johnny Bench. And he played it over and over and over.

They took Pete back to Hazard, Kentucky to bury him. After the funeral when we gathered at the Peters' home, everybody listened to the message that Johnny Bench had sent—via Marty Brennaman—to Pete.

Johnny Bench didn't know what effect he had on the life of A. N. Peters of Hazard, Kentucky. And he didn't know that even after Pete had died, the words of Johnny Bench could mean so much to so many of Pete's friends.

For eleven years Art Herring was a journeyman pitcher in the major leagues. He started with the Tigers in 1929 and pitched there five years. But he had an almost unbelievable story of a baseball prediction.

Herring grew up in Altus, Oklahoma. When Art was 12 years old in 1919, the Tiger great Ty Cobb came to Altus to visit his sister. The townspeople were so impressed by this visit that they got together a bunch of men to play baseball, just so they could see Cobb in action.

Cobb's team needed one more player. Somebody said: "Why don't you let that white-haired kid play." That kid was Art Herring. Cobb turned to the youngster and said. "You're my right fielder, son."

During the game young Art slid on his elbows and caught two line drives. Afterwards Cobb told him: "Boy, those were two of the best catches I ever saw in my life. You're going to be a big leaguer someday."

Time marched on and we come up to 1946. Herring is now pitching for the Brooklyn Dodgers. They were in St. Louis when Ty Cobb, long since retired, entered the clubhouse. Cobb visited with Durocher, Dressen, Dixie Walker, Pee Wee Reese and the other big names on the Dodgers. He started out of the clubhouse.

Art Herring stopped the great Cobb. "Mr. Cobb," he

said, "I'd like to talk with you a minute. You don't remember me, do you?"

"No," says Cobb. "I don't. There's only one Herring I
know, but he played for Milwaukee."

Then, Herring said, "Mr. Cobb, remember in 1919
when you visited your sister in Oklahoma and played a
game?"

Cobb replied, "Let me tell you about that trip. There
was a little white-haired kid who made two of the greatest catches I ever saw. I'd give anything in the world to
know where he is."

Herring beamed. "Mr. Cobb, you're looking at that kid
right now."

Cobb cornered some writers and a photographer and
the story went over the wires and back to Oklahoma.
Cobb and the white-haired kid had been reunited. Even
the great Ty Cobb couldn't forget those two catches by a
12-year-old youngster.

Stories abound about Mickey Mantle. You may remember some of the details of Mantle's boyhood. He was the
kid from Commerce, Oklahoma, trained by his dad,
Elven, or "Mutt." His dad was a worker in the zinc mines
and saw the potential in his son for everything that he
himself had wanted to be. When Mickey was just a kid—
only five or six—his dad began to train him. He taught
him to switch hit by the age of seven. He taught him
about baseball fundamentals: laying down a bunt, getting a jump on a fly ball, how to hit a cut-off man.

Mickey grew and developed into an outstanding high-
school athlete. He was banged on the shins in football
and suffered injuries that endured as long as he lasted
as a baseball player. Most observers have said that if
those injuries had not have happened, Mantle would
have been baseball's number one all-time star.

A scout discovered Mickey swatting home runs on his

local team. Mickey signed with the Yankees in 1949, right out of Commerce High School. From the minors he worked his way up and joined the Yankee team in 1951. Then he dropped back to AA where he played for the Kansas City Blues.

With Kansas City—away from the majors and away from his home and family—Mantle went into a terrible batting slump. He became discouraged and was ready to quit. Looking for sympathy, he called his dad, Mutt Mantle, the man who had nurtured him along to be a big-league star.

So, Mantle's dad drove over from Oklahoma to Kansas City. What did he do? He applied reverse psychology on Mickey.

As soon as Mutt entered Mickey's room, he went straight to the closet and started pulling out clothes.

"What are you doing?" Mickey asked.

"I'm taking you home," was the answer. "I thought I had raised a man. Now I see you ain't nothing but a coward. You can go back to Oklahoma and work in the mines with me."

"Wait a minute," said Mickey. "How 'bout another chance? Let me stay here and see if I can't get out of this slump."

His dad nodded his head, said yes and headed out of the door.

"After that," Mickey said later, "I turned it around. I pulled out of that slump and soon I was back with the Yankees in the big leagues."

What Mantle did is now in the record books. Three times he was the American League's Most Valuable Player. He hit 18 World Series home runs. He won the 1956 Triple Crown with a .353 average, 52 home runs and 130 runs batted in. In 1974 he was a unanimous selection to the Baseball Hall of Fame.

Mickey Mantle is almost 60 years old now. But he still remembers that visit from his dad in the Kansas City hotel room. And when Mutt Mantle called Mickey a coward, the youngster's reaction was to fight back, and to show his dad that he was not a quitter but a real man.

Comebacks have always been a part of baseball. And my favorite comeback story is about a favorite Tiger, John Hiller.

Hiller was probably Canada's most valuable export to the Tigers. He pitched sandlot ball in Scarborough, Ontario and was signed by the great Tiger scout Cy Williams. Cy saw him pitch one game and offered John $400 a week. Cy also threw in a pair of spikes and an old glove. Hiller snapped at the offer.

John came through the minors and first joined the Tigers in 1965. The manager then was Charlie Dressen. Dressen put Hiller into his first game to pitch to one batter—Chicago's Gene Freese. Hiller zipped three high, fast balls past Freese and struck him out. When John came back to the dugout, Dressen said: "Gee, I didn't know you could throw that hard."

Hiller said later that he really wasn't a hard thrower, but that first appearance had him all pumped up.

Then, just six years into his Tiger career, in 1971, John thought his baseball days were over. He was only 27 years old in January 1971 when he suffered a massive heart attack.

He spent five weeks in the hospital. His doctors said that he would never play baseball again. In April of '71 Hiller had surgery. Doctors removed seven feet of his intestines and cleared his arteries. By November he was running, swimming and exercising when he could. He quit drinking and smoking and vowed to himself to defy all those experts who told him he'd never pitch again.

The Tigers were concerned about Hiller and his health. First they brought him back as their batting practice pitcher. Then manager Billy Martin gave him a chance to pitch. Billy took left-hander Les Cain and Hiller to the bullpen. Cain was trying to come back after arm trouble; Hiller, after his heart attack.

Billy said to the two of them: "I'll watch you guys warm up here in the bullpen, and I'll pick one to stay on the team and release the other one."

He selected Hiller. And in July 1972 Hiller was pitching again in the big leagues. He went on to become the best relief pitcher in Tiger history. His best seasons were 1973 and '74. In '73 he was 10 and 5 with 38 saves—at that time an American League record. The next year he notched 17 victories and was picked for the American League All-Star squad.

After the 1980 season, Hiller retired. Hiller's 15-year career, all with the Tigers, was a good one, and now he's helping young, hope-to-be Tiger pitchers as he coaches them in the minors. There is a lot John can tell them about pitching technique; but he can impart even more to those youngsters about fighting back against all kinds of odds.

Some of the hardest workers on the major-league scene are the men in charge of the clubhouses. They are also the most dedicated and sometimes the most abused.

Many times a clubhouse man suffers indignities at the hands of spoiled players. Unreasonable demands and verbal abuse are commonplace. Most of the men suffer in silence—but not all.

During a night game about 10 years ago, the visiting team (not the Tigers) was getting banged around by the Brewers in Milwaukee. Their relief ace was one of the main targets of Brewer bats. Kayoed from the game in the eighth inning, he stormed into the clubhouse. Clubhouse man Jim Ksicinski was busy with his chores and paid no attention as the star proceeded to pour vodka and lime juice into the spread of food Jim had prepared for the players' post-game enjoyment.

Later, when the game was over and the players began to eat, they couldn't stomach the adulterated food. Ksicinski quietly investigated. He confronted the pitching star.

"Oh," said the pitcher, "I was just kidding around. Can't you take a joke?"

"Not one like that," Ksicinski answered.

He went immediately to the pitcher's locker and began to rip up the pitcher's sport coat and slacks. The pitcher rushed toward Jim.

"What are you doing . . . you can't do that."

"Now, now," Jim said, "can't you take a joke?"

It wasn't over. The next day the pitcher contacted the Milwaukee County officials and filed a charge that the clubhouse food was contaminated. The charge was later dismissed. Also, he talked to his teammates, urging them not to tip Ksicinski for his service during the series.

He got nowhere with that plea. As a matter of fact, when the team members filed out of the clubhouse after the final game of the series, all of them contributed to the largest amount of money that team had ever given to clubhouse man Jim Ksicinski. That says it all about how the team members felt about their spoiled pitcher, and how they felt about a clubhouse man who fought back from indignity and abuse.

Back in the '70s, a lady on Long Island wrote a letter to New York sportswriter Dick Young. Here's the way the letter went:

"The youngest of my six children is a boy named Jerome. He is seven years old. Right now he is in the baseball card phase. The other day he came to me and said he had two brothers in his cards but they play on different teams. I asked their names and he said Downing.

"In all my years as a baseball fan, I couldn't recall any mention of Al Downing having a brother in the big leagues. I asked my son to show me the cards.

"He produced one of Al Downing, the other of Brian Downing and he said, 'See, they are brothers, their last names are the same.'

"I looked at them and said to him, 'No, they couldn't be brothers because one is black and one is white.' He studied them very carefully, and then, puzzled, he said, 'Oh, I never noticed that, but can't they be brothers anyway?'

"I just thought Jerome's innocent eyes would be a wonderful way for all of us to see the world."

People all over the world remember him as a man who made millions laugh. Detroiters remember him as a man who grew up in Toledo and came to this city many times as a performer. He was also the owner of the Kansas City team in the old American Association, a one-time TV baseball announcer, and a tremendous baseball fan. I knew the great movie comedian Joe E. Brown as a warm human being, and a friend to many—especially the servicemen of World War II.

Many years ago I asked Joe what was his one most memorable moment in show business. Joe told me of a time he was entertaining the troops in the South Pacific. He had lost a son in that war, and the servicemen meant something special to him. Here's the way Joe E. Brown told it:

"I was up at three in the morning and went with some guys on a bombing mission. I came back, hopped on another plane and flew 500 miles to entertain about 2,500 soldiers. There was a homemade stage—just a few boards on top of oil drums.

"I did pantomime and routines and told jokes. I was on more than an hour. I was dead tired. I begged off doing any more. But they kept applauding. They wouldn't let me stop.

"I explained how tired I was, told them they'd heard everything I'd perfected in a lifetime of show business, but they wouldn't give up.

"Finally a youngster about 19 yelled out: 'Hey, Joe, can't you tell us some dirty stories?'

"When that kid shouted, the entire jungle must have heard it. There was complete silence. And that silence stunned me. But I recovered and I spoke directly to that kid.

"And here's what I told him: 'Son, I want your applause. A comedian like me lives on applause and laughter. I want your laughs more than you ever want me to make you laugh. But, if telling a dirty story is the price I have to pay for your laughter, I don't want it. I've never done an act I couldn't do in front of my mother and I never will.'

"When I said that," (and remember this is Joe E. Brown talking), "when I said that, these soldiers rocked that jungle with more applause than I'd ever heard anywhere—in my whole lifetime in show business.

"And that's the applause I could never forget."

On June 17, 1942, the Boston Braves' Paul Waner hit a ground ball to short. The shortstop bobbled the ball, but the official scorer awarded Waner his 3,000th hit. Waner looked at the press box and waved off the hit. The scorer changed his scoring and called it an error. The next day, Paul Waner got his 3,000th hit —a clean one.

Canadian Bob Emslie umpired in the National League for more than 30 years. The job took such a toll on his nerves that Emslie reached the point where every hair

root in his body died. He didn't have a single hair anywhere on his body.

When Bill Klem, the old umpire and his partner, heard
about this and heard the league was going to release
Emslie, he went to the league president to plead for his
friend. Klem was told that it was Emslie's doctor who had
recommended his dismissal because of the pressures of
umpiring behind home plate.

In those days, the umps worked in pairs so the plate
assignment came around at least every other day. Klem
volunteered to take Emslie with him and to work the
plate every day and let Emslie work the bases. And that
remained the arrangement for many, many years.

TWO

Fan Fare

"I write from the viewpoint of the average fan, although,
like any average fan, I think I know more about the game
than the average fan."

Art Hill

W hen I was broadcasting baseball in Brooklyn in
1948–49, I often tried to explain the Dodger fan
to my wife, Lulu. I don't think she really understood the uniqueness of that creature until she attended
a Dodgers-Phillies game at Ebbets Field.

She had followed the Dodgers for a couple of years and
in spring training and at parties she had met the various
Dodger players and their families. Though she didn't
know a lot about runs, hits and errors, she had a certain
familiarity with the personalities of the team.

Lulu took her seat in the grandstand and in front of
her was a big, muscled fan in a T-shirt. When the Dodgers' Pee Wee Reese led off in the last of the first inning,
this fan stood up and shouted, "C'mon, you bum. Hit
one."

My wife was taken aback. She tapped the fan on his shoulder.

"I beg your pardon," she said. "Do you know Mr. Reese?"

"No, lady, why?"

"If you knew him, I think you'd find him a very nice gentleman."

"Awright, lady, I'll lay off him if he's a friend of yours," was the fan's reply.

The next Brooklyn batter was Billy Cox. As he moved into the batter's box, the loudmouthed fan jumped to his feet again and shouted, "You're a bum, Cox. Do somethin'. You're nothin' but a bum."

Once again my wife tapped the man. This time before she could say anything, he whirled around.

"Is this bum a friend of yours too, lady?"

Lulu nodded.

"And what about the other bums on this team?" he asked.

"I know almost all the players," she answered.

After that answer, the fan jammed his scorecard into his hip pocket and began to walk away. Before he'd taken three steps he turned and said to my wife:

"Look, lady, I'm moving. I came out here to root my bums to a win, and I ain't gonna let you sit here behind me and spoil my whole afternoon."

The structure of baseball would collapse without fans. If they don't pay to see the games, we are all out of work. Let's examine the word "fan." It's been said that the owner of the old St. Louis Browns, Chris von Der Ahe was the inventor of that word. He called his 1880s' customers "fanatics," and gradually reduced it to "fans."

More popular words for baseball followers in the early 1900s were "bugs," or "cranks." Now, fans seems to be the universal word.

I've seen a lot of different fans in my career. They come in all colors, shapes and sizes. Each city has its own crowd characteristics. And each crowd has its own characters. Now that TV dominates the sporting scene, we see a lot more fan participation or exhibitionism. Guys with banners and painted faces and all kinds of tricks and gimmicks to get themselves before the camera.

Yet, even in pre-TV times there were avid fans. When I worked in Atlanta in the 1940s—my first baseball play-by-play job—there was a lady there named Pearl Sandow who had her own special spot in the stands and came out every game to root for the Crackers. When the city went "big-time" and the Crackers gave way to the National League Braves, Pearl was still the loyal rooter. And the Braves recognized her by giving her a special seat and commemorating that spot with a bronze plaque.

In Brooklyn—my next baseball stop—there were plenty of characters, among them Hilda Chester, who rang a cow bell at every game; and Shorty Laurice, who conducted the Brooklyn Symphony—a bunch of fans who also played musical instruments. Then there was the guy who brought helium balloons to every game and launched them as a salute to the Dodger player, Cookie Lavagetto.

Hilda Chester, the bell lady, later defected to the New York Giants. There she could root for the Giants along with another avid supporter named Louie Kleppel. Louie was an unemployed furniture mover who graced the Polo Grounds bleachers. He was better known as "Books," since he always carried three or four books with him.

Louie was the maitre d' of the bleachers. One year—1951 —he took up a collection for each Giant player and bought each one a watch. The season ran out on him before he'd presented a watch to Whitey Lockman. Louie caught the bus to Charlotte, North Carolina, rang Whitey's doorbell early one morning in October and gave a surprised Mrs. Lockman the watch for her husband. Then he caught the bus back to New York.

When I went to Baltimore, the Orioles were new to the big leagues and didn't seem to attract many eccentric fans. Later, a cab driver named Bill Hagy came along and began to lead the cheers and help bring a lot more color and excitement to the Orioles and to Memorial Stadium.

Detroit has many great fans. The best known in recent years is Joe Diroff, better known as "The Brow." Joe's a great cheerleader. Whenever the Tigers fly home, he's there to meet us. It might be cold and rainy and four in the morning, but Joe Diroff is there with his signs and a smile on his face. Joe's a retired school teacher who loves to cheer and cheer loudly.

Once at Metro Airport, Joe was leading a loud Tiger cheer as two businessmen were trying to talk on the telephone. They yelled for him to shut up. The Tiger players shouted back to quiet the businessmen while The Brow completed his cheerleading.

Yes, baseball couldn't survive without its fans.

Collecting is almost a disease. Believe me, I know because I did it for a long time. I contracted the malady when I was only 10 years old and it held me in its grip for almost 40 years.

How does a collector get started? In my case, baseball guides did it. I saw an ad in the *Sporting News* where Charlie White wanted to sell some guides. Charlie was one of the old-time statisticians. In fact, he compiled Charlie White's *Little Red Book,* which was a forerunner of the modern-day record books and appeared in the Spalding baseball guides. Anyway, Charlie had some duplicate guides for sale, and I wrote and asked for information.

Eventually, I bought a whole series of guides from him. The Reach and Spaldings ran from around 1910 through

1917. Also, there were some old Beadles and DeWitts, which had been issued in the 1860s and 1870s. (Beadle was the man who started the famous dime novel.) These older guides sold for only a dime.

I paid Charlie White $32 for the whole bunch. At that time, I had a paper route for the *Atlanta Georgian* and was making $2 per week. This was at the zenith of the Depression, and my parents thought I was absolutely zonkers to buy those old books for such an exorbitant price.

But I fooled them. In about four months there was another ad in the *Sporting News*. This time a Mr. Edwards of St. Louis wanted to buy guides. He was connected with a brokerage firm there.

I wrote him and told him what I had. Mr. Edwards wired me an offer. (It was the first telegram I had ever received.) I agreed and sold a portion—a rather small portion—of the guides I had bought from Charlie White. I received $75 for the lot.

So, I had more than doubled my money. And, naturally, I considered myself quite an astute businessman.

With the guides I kept, I had a basis on which to build my collection. And then I went at it, buying and swapping and acquiring, until I gave it all up when I moved to Florida for my winter home in 1965.

Needless to say, my first sale did make me feel great at the time. But, looking back, I must recall that just one of those many guides that I sold in a batch for $75 is worth more than twice that total price on the present-day market.

There's an old gag that I use about my mail. I say that Paul Carey and I get a lot of letters at Tiger Stadium. Some of them are very kind—the rest we turn over to the FBI. Guess there is a word or two of truth there.

One of my longtime friendships developed through the

mail. When I first started broadcasting, I did a 15-minute radio sports show on WSB-Atlanta. I was fresh out of college and brand new to the business. I was merely feeling my way along. I did some interviews, but mostly I wrote features and used them. I did background stories, essays, a series on Georgians in the big leagues, and some recaps of sports history.

Naturally, I was concerned about what kind of reaction I was getting. The bosses at the station seemed satisfied, and I began to get some mail—most of it favorable. But a letter to me early in my career had a profound influence on me. It came from a man in Wapakoneta, Ohio, which was a long distance from Atlanta. First of all, I was thrilled that anybody that far away was listening to me, and also proud that he took the time and effort to write. Not only did Mr. Lutz write to me, he also wrote a letter about my program to the editor of the *Sporting News*. This letter was published in the *Sporting News* and was probably the first recognition I'd ever been accorded outside my native state of Georgia.

I answered that letter from Franlau Lutz. He continued to write, and we struck up a real friendship through the mail. That was 1940. He kept writing to me until he died 50 years later.

In the course of our correspondence, I discovered that Franlau was a shut-in. He had suffered for years with polio, and sports was his number one diversion. We wrote back and forth over the years, but never met in person.

Then one day just a few years ago, his daughter, who lives in the Detroit area, wrote me that she was bringing her Dad to a Tiger game, and perhaps we could get together. I left the booth, went down into the stands and had a beautiful visit with my longtime friend.

Two years ago, he came again to visit his daughter, and my wife, Lulu, and I went over to his daughter's house for a family dinner with Franlau. We had a great time, and I'll never forget our friendship, which lasted all those years.

Broadcasting these games has a lot of rewards for me, but none greater than the privilege of making friends with the fans who are out there listening and sometimes writing to me at Tiger Stadium.

We still hear a lot about the Tiger greats: Ty Cobb, Mickey Cochrane, Charlie Gehringer, Hank Greenberg and the other Hall of Famers. But one of the most popular Tigers of all time is seldom mentioned. And yet, when this star was traded away from Detroit in the mid-'30s there was a louder outcry than there has been following any other Tiger deal. His name: Gerald "Gee" Walker.

Walker couldn't hold his own with the other Tigers we just mentioned, but in popularity he had no peer. Gee was a good player, no more than that. An impulsive man from the word "go," Gee Walker was erratic in the field, a poor base-runner, a better-than-fair hitter. He made more mistakes on his own than the rest of the team combined. And yet he was idolized by the Tiger fans.

Gee could do no wrong. The average guy identified with him. We don't look for perfection, I guess. We want our heroes like ourselves—full of faults. And Gee Walker fitted into that pattern.

An incident in the 1934 World Series, which pitted the Tigers against the St. Louis Cardinals, capsulized Gee's entire career in baseball. Walker came to bat in the ninth inning and singled in the tying run of the game. The Tigers eventually went on to beat the Cards in extra innings that afternoon.

Here was the thrill of a lifetime for this colorful young man from Mississippi. As he stood on first base and heard the cheers, he was on top of the world.

Then the players on the Cardinal bench began to yell

at Gee. They called him names, they kidded him about his crazy antics. He turned to listen and yell back, and just at that moment Card catcher Bill DeLancey fired the ball to first baseman Rip Collins. Collins quickly tagged out Walker and the hero had been picked off first—a typical scene in the life of Gerald Walker.

Earlier that season on the road, Gee had been caught off base twice on one play. These lapses so infuriated manager Cochrane that he sent Walker back to Detroit. He called a meeting of the players and put it up to them whether Walker would remain with the team or be sent away. The players voted for Gee to stay, but Mickey suspended him for 10 days and never forgave him.

Yet, the fans still loved Walker. He was more popular than ever. Gee was a Tiger for seven years, and when he was dealt off to Chicago, newspapers were flooded with indignant letters. The barrage continued for weeks—the greatest outcry of its sort in Tiger history. Here was a man who could do no wrong. Certainly not a great player, Gee Walker was truly one of the most popular in all of Tiger history.

Just about everybody who ever played major-league baseball has had a hero. When the present-day stars were youngsters, they worshipped certain other stars and dreamed of someday taking their places.

Even the great Ty Cobb had a hero. In fact, he had two of them.

Ty's first hero was Nap Lajoie. When the American League started in 1902, Lajoie was its number-one star. A French-Canadian hack driver, he was tall and handsome. On the diamond he was one of baseball's most graceful performers. He had played for the Philadelphia National League team for seven years before he jumped to the new league. Second base was his position, and nobody played it better.

Lajoie was a great hitter. In one season he batted .422

and rounded off his 21-year career with a lifetime mark of .338. He was the idol of millions of American kids, including a youngster from Royston, Georgia, named Ty Cobb.

When Ty was 16 he saw his first big-league team in action. And it was Lajoie's team, the Cleveland Indians. But on that spring afternoon in Atlanta, another hero took the place of Lajoie in the heart of young Cobb.

The Indians were training that spring of 1903 in Atlanta and played their games at old Piedmont Park. Cobb talked his father into letting him take the train to Atlanta to see the Indians in action.

He went straight from the downtown railroad station to the ballpark. It was long before game time, and the Indians were practicing. Ty wandered into the park and sat in the left-field bleachers. He was there all alone in the hot Georgia sun.

Suddenly he looked up and saw a big, husky Cleveland player standing at the fence and looking at him. The big guy spoke:

"Hiya, kid. What's your name?"

"Tyrus Cobb."

"Where you from?"

"Royston, Georgia."

"Where's that?"

"Oh, 'bout 100 miles from here."

"Well, my name's Bill Bradley. Glad to meet you."

It was the Indians' star third baseman, Bill Bradley. And just like that he was Ty Cobb's new hero.

Bradley noticed a camera in Ty's lap and asked him if he'd like to have his picture and some pictures of his teammates. For the next several minutes the young fan was taking snapshots of the Indian players.

Cobb said many years later, "I kept those pictures until they were almost dust. Twenty-six years after that, I saw Bradley at a banquet. I reminded him of that day in Atlanta.

"He had a hard time believing I was the timid kid from Royston who took his picture. But it's the truth."

Yes, even Ty Cobb had a hero. He had two. Nap Lajoie at first; and then along came a friendly man named Bill Bradley. And Bradley turned out to be Cobb's number-one idol.

There was a sidelight to a Tiger home game not long ago that had a profound effect on me. You didn't read about it in the sports section, it didn't affect that season's pennant race, and the incident won't be included even in the most obscure baseball statistics.

Actually, it was a crowd response to a trivia question— but it took an interesting and delightful turn. Early in the game the trivia question had been posted on Lew Matlin's informative scoreboard—something about who was the last major leaguer to bat in more than 100 runs in a season and hit less than 10 home runs. Answer: sixth inning.

When the sixth inning rolled around, so did the answer: George Kell. When his name was posted, the whole stadium looked to the TV booth, stood and cheered George Kell.

How many times does a crowd of almost 50,000 cheer an obscure statistic? Not many, but this was different. They were cheering for something else. The crowd was cheering George Kell, Hall-of-Fame player; George Kell, longtime Tiger TV announcer; and George Kell, good and decent man.

That Tiger crowd was telling Kell that they all loved him. Just a few nights before, a slip of the tongue on a telecast had embarrassed George. But the crowd was saying, "Don't worry about it, George. It can happen to anybody."

And over the years Kell has been overshadowed somewhat by his younger TV partner, Al Kaline—a man of superstar status and also a Hall of Famer, elected several years before George was voted in.

Yet, in a beautiful and spontaneous way, the big Tiger crowd was saying, "George, we're cheering you because we love you. You're a good man and you belong to us."

Before 1921, fans were required to return foul balls. At Pittsburgh that year, a fan named Reuben Berman shocked the baseball world by keeping a ball. Team owners took Berman to court and lost. The court ruled fans could keep baseballs.

During a rain delay, the radio announcer said, "The game has been held up by rain. The score is 5–5, and Jack Smith is on second." He repeated the announcement a couple of times and a lady phoned, "Why do they keep that poor Mr. Smith on second base in all this rain? He will catch his death of cold."

A Catholic priest was bothered at a game by a talkative baseball fan who kept asking ridiculous questions. The priest bought a hot dog from a vendor. The vendor handed the hot dog to the fan who had been bothering the priest and the fan passed it along to the priest who gulped down the hot dog. It was the first time a hot dog had ever gone from the prying fan into the friar.

THREE

Diamonds in the Rough

"All I have is natural ability."

Mickey Mantle

Baseball, like life, is full of ironies. But one of the most ironic incidents of the game is the fact that Ty Cobb, baseball's meanest man, was started in the profession by a Sunday school teacher.

Cobb, regarded by most as the greatest player who ever lived, was sorely lacking in principles. He wanted to win, and that was all that mattered. To reach the next base he would slice his grandmother with his spikes—that's how mean he was.

Well, when Ty was just a youngster in Royston, Georgia, his life was influenced by a big red-haired Southern minister and Sunday school teacher named John Yarborough. Yarborough had been a fine schoolboy catcher in Augusta, and when he was assigned the little church in Royston, he found a group of teenage baseball-minded boys who never came to church. Cobb was one of them.

Still, the boys knew that Yarborough had been a ball-player and they asked him to coach their team—the Royston Rompers.

He made a deal: If the boys would come to church, he would coach. And right away Reverend Yarborough saw the potential in young Cobb. Also, about that time Ty changed his boyhood ambition from wanting to be a doctor to wanting to be a ballplayer.

He asked the minister to help him get started in professional baseball. Cobb's father didn't like the idea, but Reverend Yarborough talked to him and persuaded him to consent to Ty's going into the game.

Ty was only 17 at the time. He had written to the Augusta club but had received no answers. Then Reverend Yarborough got busy. He knew some of the Augusta club's officials, so he wrote them and recommended Cobb. The answer came back for the young man to report.

Cobb reported in the spring of 1904. He paid his own expenses and took with him a letter from Yarborough saying he was a good boy and a good ballplayer. He hit a home run in his first game on a ball the manager told him to bunt. He showed inexperience in the outfield and failed to hit in the second game. Ty Cobb was immediately released . . . just like that.

But he had made his start and he was to come back later and flash across the baseball sky like no other ever has. Baseball's best player, baseball's greatest competitor—that was Ty Cobb. The meanest of them all got his start through the kindness of a Methodist minister and Sunday school teacher.

Frank J. Navin—more than any single individual—was responsible for Ty Cobb getting his chance to play in the major leagues. And, when Cobb became baseball's greatest player, he contributed toward making Navin a rich and influential force in the game.

In 1905 Navin was still new to baseball. A former book-keeper, he had become part-owner of the Tigers only the year before. The Tigers trained in Augusta, Georgia that spring of 1905, and Navin made a trip to their camp.

When the part-owner of the Tigers entered the lobby of Augusta's Hotel Albion, he was greeted by "Wild" Bill Donovan, Detroit pitcher and a man who was to become one of Navin's lifetime favorites. With Donovan was Detroit's second baseman Herman "Germany" Schaefer. After a word or two about the Augusta weather and how the Tigers looked, Schaefer began to tell Navin about a youngster who was playing for the Augusta team.

"Say, this Augusta club we've been playing has a new kid who's a scream," he said to Navin. "Wait'll you see him. He'll give you enough laughs for the whole season. He tries to stretch every single into a double and every double into a triple. He starts for second when the pitcher's holding the ball. I guess he doesn't even know there's a third base, 'cause if he's on second when the batter hits a grounder to the infield, he keeps right on running to the plate. And he bunts with two strikes on him. Crazy as a bedbug."

"What's his name?" asked Navin.

"Cobb," answered Schaefer. "You'll see him tomorrow and laugh yourself sick. Don't let him see you laughing or it'll spoil the fun. We've had a great time kidding him along. If you talk to him, tell him you think he's a great ballplayer."

Next afternoon, Navin had his first look at Cobb. The youngster was different, all right. But Navin noticed that he was extremely fast and he started quickly. Navin could tell that he had raw ability but needed polish.

Navin made it a point to talk with Cobb's manager of the previous season at Augusta, George Leidy. Leidy had been succeeded as manager by Andy Roth, but had stayed with Augusta to play center field.

"I'll admit Cobb needs experience," said Leidy, "but

as he develops and gets used to playing on a team, you'll see the world's greatest ballplayer—nothing less."

The Detroit club had used Augusta's park for spring training and, instead of paying rent, Navin made a deal with the Augusta owner, William J. Croke—a common practice during those years. He agreed to lend Augusta a pitcher named Eddie Cicotte in exchange for the use of the grounds and the pick of any Augusta player for $750 when the season ended.

As the Sally League season drew to a close, the Tigers faced that choice. Which player should they pluck from the Augusta roster? Navin favored the selection of Clyde Engle. Navin's manager, Bill Armour, preferred Cobb. Armour was basing his choice on recommendations from three trusted sources: Sally League umpire Bill Byron, scout Heinie Youngman and George Leidy.

Armour convinced Navin that Cobb should be the pick. Navin completed the purchase. Ty reported to the Tigers August 30, 1905 at old Bennett Park. He was a dynamic symbol of Detroit until 1927 when he was released and signed with the Philadelphia Athletics.

Ty played for only two owners, Navin and Connie Mack. He was an employee of Navin for 22 years, and spent his final two years under Mack.

The fact that Armour had touted Cobb was important to Ty's success. Armour had to let the youngster play in order to vindicate his judgment. Under other circumstances, Cobb might not have stayed in the lineup.

Cobb's early years were not easy. The Tiger players remembered him as "that crazy ballplayer." They ridiculed Navin for making the deal. Also, manager Armour began to waiver on his choice of Cobb.

Then Navin made a maneuver which paid dividends for Cobb. He fired Armour, who couldn't appreciate the unorthodox daring of this wild rookie. He hired as his new manager Hughie Jennings, a former Baltimore Oriole. When American League president Ban Johnson heard of Navin's plans, he wired him:

"We don't want any of that roughneck Baltimore crowd in our league."

Navin stood his ground. He told Johnson that if Jennings were not allowed to manage the Tigers, William H. Yawkey (Navin's rich partner) would withdraw his financial support. Jennings stayed, Cobb played and the rest, as they say, is history.

Twenty-some years ago, when Sam Mele was the manager of the Minnesota Twins, his team was in a terrific batting slump. About the same time, Sam's good friend and Minnesota scout Del Wilber was out on the prowl, looking for prospective big-league talent.

Wilber came across a wonderful young pitcher—even more wonderful than he had ever anticipated. He grabbed the young man immediately after the game, rushed him to the hotel, locked him in the room and phoned Sam Mele.

"Sam," he said. "I've landed the greatest young pitcher in the country for the Twins. I wouldn't have believed it, but I saw it myself. He struck out every man who came to bat—27 men in succession in nine innings. Only one man even fouled one off. The pitcher is right here with me now. What shall I do?"

Back came Mele's voice over the long-distance line: "Sign up the guy who got the foul. We need hitters."

Before Ted Williams hit over .400 in 1941, the last American Leaguer to do it was Harry Heilmann, the great Tiger outfielder. Harry's lifetime batting average was .342—the same as Babe Ruth's. And most baseball people consider him the second best right-hand hitter in base-ball history. (Rogers Hornsby had to be the best.)

What kind of money could Heilmann demand today? The Hall of Famer's potential would be unlimited.

How much did he make in his playing career? Not very much.

As a matter of fact, Heilmann got only a spaghetti dinner for signing his first professional contract. That's right, one spaghetti dinner.

Harry had flunked out of school and had failed to make the varsity baseball team. He went to work as a book-keeper for the Mutual Biscuit Company of San Francisco in 1913. One Saturday afternoon, he left the office and walked two blocks before he remembered he had left his coat at the office. As he returned he bumped into Jim Riordan, who was managing the Hanford team in the San Joaquin semi-pro league.

Jim needed a third baseman. Harry had never played there but agreed to try for the game the next afternoon. The pay was $10. Not only did he play, but Heilmann was the hero. He doubled in two runs in the 11th to win the game for Hanford. A scout for Portland named Jim Richardson saw the game and offered Heilmann a con-tract. Harry signed and that evening received his bo-nus—a spaghetti dinner.

That was 1913 ... Heilmann played that year for Port-land in the Northwestern League and batted .305 in 122 games. The league president was Fielder Jones, who also scouted for the Tigers. He recommended to Tiger owner Frank Navin that Detroit draft Heilmann, along with Carl Mays and Dave Bancroft. Navin drafted Heilmann and Mays but Bancroft was grabbed by the Phillies.

Harry's first Tiger contract called for $350 per month. He was paid $2,100 for the entire American League sea-son. He played first base and outfield, batting .225.

When he received a contract for the same terms next spring, Heilmann balked. San Francisco had offered him

$450 more per month, if he could get out of his Tiger contract. The Tigers wouldn't let him go, but did farm him to San Francisco, where he hit .364.

The next year, 1916, Heilmann was in the majors again and never returned to the minors. His Tiger career lasted through 1929 and he played two more years with the Reds before he quit.

It was a great career. Four times he won the batting title, with averages of .394, .403, .393 and .398.

What money he could command now! But he was ahead of his time. Heilmann had to be content with a good living, diamond fame, a host of friends and a spaghetti dinner bonus.

When young Stan Musial was growing up in Donora, Pennsylvania, he was struggling with a problem. His high school days were almost over and Stan's dad wanted him to go to college. Several colleges had bid for his athletic services, but Stan's dad felt that he should accept a basketball scholarship from the University of Pittsburgh.

Stan didn't want to go to college. He wanted to play professional baseball. So around the Musial dinner table there was a constant debate on the subject.

Then a young lady entered the domestic drama. She was Miss Helen Kloz, the high school librarian. She recognized the problem bothering young Musial and gave him some words of advice.

"Stan," she told the youngster, "I realize how badly you want to go into professional baseball. It's plain to see that you want baseball more than a college education. Being in education myself, I believe in it, but I also know that you must follow your heart."

Musial followed that advice. His dad understood and gave Stan his permission, and the world came to know the diamond greatness of Stan Musial.

Throughout their history the Tigers have not been strong on pitching. Hitters generally have dominated the Tiger story over the years. Yet, the Detroit organization missed out on three Hall of Fame pitchers who could have turned the team's history around: Walter Johnson, Carl Hubbell and Bob Feller.

Hubbell did belong to the Tigers in the late '20s, but they cut him loose, and he later reached stardom with the New York Giants. Johnson and Feller were touted to the Tigers, but the organization overlooked each of them. Here's the inside story on the Feller case.

Bob Feller and his cousin Hal Manders were pitching for the Farmers' Union team of Des Moines, Iowa in 1935. Bob won 17 games and lost three; Hal, who later pitched for the Tigers, won 14 and lost one that season. In June, a Farmers' Union official named L. M. Peet wrote to Steve O'Rourke, a Detroit scout, telling him that he had two likely looking pitchers on his team—referring to Feller and Manders. He invited O'Rourke to come to Des Moines to take a look.

O'Rourke never showed. Then another employee of the Farmers' Union wrote to Cy Slapnicka of Cleveland and told him about Feller. He gave him the same information that O'Rourke had received. Slapnicka hurried to Des Moines and saw Feller pitch. That same July afternoon in 1935 he signed Feller and gave him a $500 bonus, asking Bob and his dad to promise to keep the transaction a secret so Bob could finish the season as an amateur. Slapnicka promised Feller he would assign him to Fargo, North Dakota in the Northern League the following spring.

Feller continued to pitch in the summer of '35 for the Farmers' Union team. He and Manders pitched the team to the Iowa state championship. Then the team went on to Battle Creek for the national tournament.

Manders didn't go to Battle Creek. Instead, he enrolled at the University of Iowa. But Feller did go, and he dazzled the scouts there. Bob pitched against a Georgia team and lost, 1–0, but he fanned 18 batters.

Among the scouts was Steve O'Rourke, the Detroit scout who earlier had ignored Feller. He was impressed by Bullet Bob. So much so, that he wanted to sign him. He talked to Feller's dad. But Mr. Feller was sworn to secrecy and couldn't tell O'Rourke that Bob had already signed with Cleveland. The Tiger scout offered the Fellers $10,000 for Bob's signature. Earlier O'Rourke could have had Feller for $500, or maybe even for nothing. But now, it was too late.

Feller refused to go to Fargo the next spring. Slapnicka shifted him to the Cleveland farm club in New Orleans. He wouldn't go there, either. So, Slapnicka brought him to Cleveland to pitch for the Richmond Clothiers. Whenever the Indians were home, Bob would work out with them.

He got his first chance in an exhibition game against the St. Louis Cardinals. Bob was 17 at the time. Two weeks later he was pitching for the Indians in the American League. He made his first start against the Browns, fanned 15 and beat 'em 4–1. He went on to become one of baseball's great pitchers. He won 266 games, but missed more baseball at his peak because of war service than any other star. Bob served in the U.S. Navy for almost four baseball seasons, winning eight battle stars. Still, he was a shoo-in for the Hall of Fame before he reached his 44th birthday.

The Tigers passed up another of baseball's greatest pitchers because the Tiger owner wouldn't listen to the words of a cigar salesman.

This story goes back to the early 1900s. William H. Yawkey and Frank Navin were partners in the Tiger ownership. Yawkey was the money man; Navin ran the club. At that time, a young man who worked for the telephone company in Weiser, Idaho was pitching semi-pro ball and attracting local attention.

A traveling cigar salesman (whose name is lost to history) saw the phenom in action and began to send a series of letters about the youngster to the only man he knew in baseball—Bill Yawkey. Yawkey passed the letters along to his partner, Frank Navin.

"Who is this guy who keeps writing?" asked Navin.

"He's a friend of mine," Yawkey told him. "A cigar salesman. Gets around the country a lot, and he knows his baseball."

Then Navin came up with a costly observation: "If he knows so much about baseball, what's he doing peddling cigars?"

So, Navin stuffed away the letter in his desk and forgot all about it. Meanwhile, the cigar salesman wouldn't give up. He next directed his bombardment of letters about the pitching phenom to the Washington Senators. They paid attention. Washington dispatched Cliff Blankenship, an injured catcher, to take a look at the telephone worker who was causing such literary inspiration. Blankenship went to Idaho and saw the youngster lose, 1–0, in 12 innings on an error. But he knew the letter-writing cigar salesman was right.

So, he whipped out a $100 bill as a bonus and offered the raw young pitcher $350 per month to join the Washington Senators for the rest of the 1907 season.

In August 1907, that one-time telephone worker became a big-league pitcher. Just three months short of his 20th birthday, he made his debut against the pennant-bound Detroit Tigers, the team that had ignored him.

Before the next season was over, the youngster was famous. In 1908 he pitched three shutouts in four days against New York. In the 10 seasons from 1910 to 1919, he won 25, 25, 32, 36, 28, 27, 25, 23, 23 and 20 games.

And he pitched all those years with the Washington Senators, a team that played .500 ball or better only 10 times in the pitcher's 21 seasons. He racked up 416 victories in the American League and fanned more than 200 batters for seven straight years.

This was the telephone worker who had been recommended by a traveling cigar salesman ... the young phenom the Tigers passed up ... the great Walter Johnson.

There's an old saying in baseball that goes this way: "You win some, you lose some, and some are rained out." This bit of sweat-shirt philosophy pertains to games, of course. But I can think of one player who was won by the Yankees and lost by another club because *he* was, so to speak, rained out.

The name is Mantle—Mickey Mantle. The great star might have been a St. Louis Brown (and later maybe a Baltimore Oriole when that team succeeded the Browns) except for a rainy 1949 day in St. Louis.

Back in those days, Zack Taylor was managing the Browns and Mantle was a 17-year-old kid working in a lead and zinc mine in Commerce, Oklahoma. Mickey was making 80 cents an hour in the mines and picking up $15 a Sunday playing shortstop for a semi-pro team.

Mantle's high school coach had connections with the Browns. One day he brought Mickey over to St. Louis so the Browns could look him over.

But it rained for four solid hours. Finally the coach gave up and took Mantle back to Oklahoma.

Not too much later, Tom Greenwade, the Yankee scout, came to Commerce, offered Mantle $1,500 to sign, and landed him for the Yankees.

It was a long and successful journey for Mantle. From the lead and zinc mines at 80 cents an hour to a salary of $100,000 a year with the Yankees. Yet, if it hadn't rained that day in St. Louis, the history of the Browns and Mickey Mantle might have been a different story.

Brooks Robinson—Hall-of-Famer, Most Valuable Player, World Series star, 23 years with the Orioles— might never had made it to the big leagues except for a letter. An old-time pal of new Baltimore manager Paul Richards thought enough of Brooks to write Paul about him. The old-timer was Lindsay Deal, who had played for Paul on the old Atlanta Crackers.

Robby had never played high school ball. His school didn't have a team, but he was an American Legion player, and Deal liked what he had seen.

Brooks was sent to York, Pennsylvania and didn't break into the Oriole lineup until September 17, 1955. He was a last-minute choice to start at third base because Kal Segrist had become ill. In his second time at bat against Washington he got his first hit —a single off left-hander Chuck Stobbs. After Brooks went 2 for 4 in that game, he called his dad and told him he didn't think the big leagues were so tough after all.

Then, the big leagues caught up with him—he went 0 for 18 the rest of the year.

There were times when it looked as if he might not make the grade. He was a poor hitter in those early years. But he worked hard and by the time he hung up the spikes, he had become one of the best.

Sterling (Sheriff) Fowble was a scout for the New York Mets. He scoured the territory on the East Coast, always on the lookout for a phenom—that rare find who could turn a team from a poor finisher into a pennant contender.

One afternoon, Sheriff thought he had found his man. A youngster had called him on the phone with glowing reports on himself. And Sheriff had arranged a meeting.

He was pleased to see a tall, well-built youngster about 18 years old.

"All right son," said Fowble, "tell me about yourself."

"Well, Mr. Fowble," was the answer, "I think I can make it with the Mets. In school I set a record in the high jump. I made the all-state teams in football and basketball, and I run the 100 in less than 10 seconds. In baseball I pitch and play first. I won 14 games and lost none and hit .475 this season."

Fowble was ecstatic. He rubbed his hands together and then spoke. "Sounds like there's nothing wrong with you."

"Well, there's only one thing," said the hot prospect. "I do lie a little."

Baseball's first scout was Harry Wright, who in the 1880s visited California in search of talent for Philadelphia. He found two stars there: Jim Fogarty and Tom Brown.

The expression "good field and no hit" was originated by Mike Gonzales of the Cardinals when he scouted Moe Berg.

Sometimes teams give up on a player too early. Connie Mack of the A's had "Shoeless" Joe Jackson for two years, playing him in only 10 games. Then Mack traded him to Cleveland for Briscoe Lord and cash. Jackson went on to hit .408, .395 and .373 in his first three seasons as a regular.

FOUR

New Kids on the Block

"Don't look back, something might be gaining on you."
Leroy "Satchel" Paige

The assault of Hank Aaron on the home-run record of Babe Ruth was one of the most exciting baseball dramas of our time. Aaron's 755 career homers eclipsed the Babe's 714 and ensured Henry a lasting spot in baseball history.

But it was as a rookie that Aaron turned one of the niftiest phrases of his long career. In those days, Hank was a man of few words and usually they were direct and to the point.

He came to the plate one afternoon holding the bat so the trademark did not point up, as most hitters hold it.

"Say," said a veteran catcher to Hank, "you're up here at the plate with the trademark down ... you should be holding that bat with the trademark up, so you can read it."

Hank turned to the catcher and said, "I didn't come up here to read. I came up here to hit."

Some crazy things happen in big-league baseball—things that nobody can explain. Take the case of a 21-year-old rookie pitcher who baffled the great Babe Ruth just about every time he pitched to him.

The rookie was Hub Pruett. Hub was a little left-hander—5'10," weighing 165 lbs.—who'd just come off the campus of the University of Missouri to pitch for the St. Louis Browns in 1922.

That year Babe Ruth came to bat 13 times against Pruett, and the left-hander struck Ruth out 10 of those 13 times. The Browns almost beat the Yankees for the American League pennant that year, and certainly Pruett was one of the reasons they came so close. He won seven games and saved seven more. And he won two out of his three decisions against the mighty Yankees.

The first time Pruett faced Ruth in May, he threw a curve past him and struck him out. A month later, he did it again. Two days after that, he struck out the Babe three more times. That made it five in a row. In July, Ruth finally hit a Pruett pitch, but he tapped it back to the mound and was an easy out. In the same game, the Babe struck out two more times. But Pruett's arm began to hurt. He walked two batters in the sixth inning and hit another. The bases were loaded and who was coming up? The great Babe Ruth. Pruett was feeling a real twinge in his arm. He called his catcher, Hank Severeid, to the mound.

"Maybe I'd better come out," he told Severeid. "I can hardly get the ball up to the plate. Bases loaded and Ruth up there . . . ."

Hank urged the rookie to stay and pitch to Babe. Pruett did and again he struck out the mighty Yankee slugger—for the third time in the game. After that, Pruett left the game.

His arm was still hurting and he didn't pitch again in that 1922 season until August. He hadn't done a whole lot that rookie year, but already he was known as the little rookie left-hander with the jinx on Babe Ruth.

The Browns were playing the Yanks again. New York loaded the bases and Ruth was the batter. Manager Lee Fohl summoned Pruett from the bullpen to pitch once more against the Babe. He fanned Ruth for the ninth time in 11 at bats.

The race for the American League pennant moved into September. And the Browns were still in it, trailing the New Yorkers by a game and a half. The Yankees came to St. Louis for a crucial series. They beat St. Louis' best pitcher, Urban Shocker, 2–1 in the first game.

Hub Pruett started the next one. In the first inning, he fanned Ruth with a screwball on the outside corner. He fanned the Babe again in the fourth. But in the sixth, Ruth finally touched up the rookie. He hit a 2–2 pitch to deep right, far out of the park. And the Babe singled off Pruett in the ninth.

But the Brownies won that game behind their rookie left-hander. And Ruth's homer was the only run the Yankees scored. St. Louis, with its 5–1 win, had tied the series. But the Yanks were too much. They won the next game and went on to take the pennant. Hub Pruett, even with his mastery over Ruth, couldn't stop the Yankees by himself. Ruth was two for 13 against Pruett. Hub had only 70 strikeouts that year and 10 were against Ruth.

Next spring, Pruett fanned Ruth three times in their first five meetings. And he continued throughout his career to fool the Babe.

Yet, his career was only mediocre. He pitched seven years in the big leagues and never won more than seven games a season. His complete career victory total was only 29 against 48 losses, yet he was the master of baseball's greatest slugger.

There's no doubt that the great Ted Williams had tremendous ability. But he also had a large amount of determination to make himself the very best.

That determination was evident even in the first game Williams played in the major leagues. He faced the tough New York Yankee pitcher, Red Ruffing. Ruffing struck him out. The next time he batted, Williams fanned again. Ted came back to the Red Sox dugout and told pitcher Jack Wilson, "If that guy throws me the same pitch next time, I'll hit it out of the park."

The brash rookie was right—almost. The next time he batted, Ruffing threw him the same pitch. Ted swung and drove the ball to the deep reaches of right-center field. It hit the top of the fence and bounced back onto the field. Williams pulled into second base with a double— the first hit of his career. He had 2,653 more before he quit the game. And he never lost the determination that made him one of baseball's greats.

Some outstanding pitchers in the majors make stardom with two or three pitches. But Dizzy Trout, the big ex-Tiger right-hander, once had seven. Diz was just a green youngster when he reported for the first time to spring training with the Tigers at Lakeland, Florida in 1937. Catcher Mickey Cochrane was also the manager that year. Diz was quick to inform Cochrane about his versatility. "I've got seven different pitches," he told Mickey, "and every one of them is a good one. What kind of signals do you guys on the Tigers use in a game?"

Cochrane answered: "One finger for a fast ball, two for a curve, and if you think I'm going to take off my mitt and go all the way to your sixth and seventh pitches, you had better forget it right now."

For one brief moment Floyd Giebell was a big part of Tiger history. Old-timers may remember him for one game; most of the modern fans know little about him. Giebell's day was September 27, 1940—the day he pitched the Tigers to a pennant.

The Tigers were battling the Cleveland Indians in Cleveland that afternoon. Detroit led the Indians by two games in the fight for the pennant. Oscar Vitt, the Indian manager, had named his ace, Bob Feller, to open the series. Tiger manager Del Baker wanted to wait before making his selection. Baker's pitching staff was suffering from overwork. The lead between the Tigers and Cleveland had changed 17 times in three months and now the hated Yankees were pulling up close to the other two contenders.

Baker called a meeting of his team and let the players decide on the starting pitcher. They made a strange choice—Giebell, a 30-year-old rookie from Pennsboro, West Virginia. Giebell had pitched two American League games the previous year and had been recalled from Buffalo only a few days before this historic date. He had won 15 and lost 17 at Buffalo. The year before that he was 1 and 10 at Toledo.

A Ladies Day crowd of 45,000 turned out that day in Cleveland. They came with fruits and vegetables and during batting practice, began to throw all sorts of missiles at the Tigers. In the first inning, Detroit left fielder Hank Greenberg moved under a fly ball off the bat of Roy Weatherly and was doused with a shower of fruit and trash. Somehow he caught the ball.

An inning later, catcher Birdie Tebbetts was hit on the head by a basket of tomatoes, bottles and other rubbish. The game was delayed 10 minutes while the unconscious Tebbetts was taken to the Tiger dugout and revived.

Giebell, meanwhile, never seemed nervous. He kept his cool and escaped an Indian threat in the third. The

Tribe put runners on first and third in that inning with none out. But he got the next three.

Rudy York banged a two-run homer down the left-field line in the fourth to give the Tigers a 2–0 lead.

In the seventh, the Indians put on another threat, but with runners on second and third and only one out, Giebell fanned Ben Chapman and then retired Roy Weatherly on a grounder to third.

In the ninth, the rookie set the Cleveland team down 1–2–3, ending the game by getting pinch-hitter Jeff Heath on a grounder.

Giebell was mobbed by his teammates. Slugger Rudy York, who hit the winning home run, gave his bat to Giebell.

That was Floyd Giebell's moment of glory—pitching the pennant-clinching game for the Tigers. His moment didn't last long. The next year he was back in the minor leagues. And he never won another major-league game. But he had his Rudy York bat . . . and his memories.

Many say Rogers Hornsby was the best right-handed hitter who ever stepped up to the plate. But most are not aware that in one afternoon he drove a rookie pitcher right out of baseball.

The youngster's name was Lefty Williams. Paul Waner, sort of a sponsor for young Mr. Williams, brought him out of their native Oklahoma and into professional baseball. At the time of our story, both Waner and Williams were with San Francisco, and they were to play an exhibition game with the St. Louis Cards.

Before the game, the Seal players were sitting around their clubhouse talking about Hornsby and what a great hitter he was. Somebody turned to Williams, who was to pitch that day, and asked, "How you gonna pitch the great Hornsby, Lefty?"

It didn't take the cocky Mr. Williams long to answer.

"Oh, I'll pitch him tight . . . keep the ball in on him."

Well, the first time Hornsby came to bat, Williams shot a fast one toward the inside. Hornsby stepped back, swung and lined the ball over the left-field fence.

On the bench in the next inning, Williams told his teammates. "Don't worry, next time I'm pitching him outside. That'll get him."

So, the next time he curved the great Hornsby. The pitch started toward the outside corner, but it ended up over the right-field fence—another Hornsby home run.

In his third at bat, Rogers rapped a down-the-middle fastball on a sharp line into center and had to settle for a single.

That was the last pitch the cocky Mr. Williams made in that game. He walked from the mound and to the showers.

Waner said that Williams was no good from that day on. He was never again a pitcher. The opposition began to ride him whenever he took the mound, yelling, "Hey Lefty, how do you pitch to Hornsby?"

That barb always got to him. Williams, the once-cocky youngster, lost all his confidence, and his pitching ability was lost along with it. The great Hornsby was the un- knowing villain in the whole affair, with three vicious drives, knocking Lefty Williams out of baseball.

Did you ever hear the story about the pitcher who was literally drummed out of the major leagues? Harry Cov- eleski was a 22-year-old rookie in 1908, pitching for the Philadelphia Phillies. The Phillies were going nowhere that season, but the Giants were headed for a pennant— until they encountered their trouble with Harry. He beat the mighty Giants three times in a five-game series and helped to knock them out of the championship.

Here's what the *New York Herald* of Monday, October 5, 1908, said: "If the Giants lose the pennant, Coveleski deserves the credit for defeating them. Last summer he was hurling for an amateur team in Wildwood, New Jersey, having graduated from a coal miners' aggregation. He was picked out of the Jersey marshes and is very green. Earlier this year the Giants drubbed him, 14–2."

The Giants managed to come back and tie the Cubs for the title, but then lost to Chicago in a playoff. Giant manager John McGraw said that the rookie Coveleski was the one man who beat the Giants out of the pennant. McGraw couldn't stand to lose. And he vowed to get even with the rookie pitcher.

The next year, 1909, when Coveleski was pitching against the Giants, McGraw was coaching at third. As soon as Harry took to the mound, McGraw began to pace back and forth in the coach's box and shout "boom-boom-boom-boom," imitating the beat of a drum. He kept it up and would not relent.

Harry Coveleski lost his cool. His nerves were shot and he couldn't get the ball over the plate. He was a walking disaster. Never again did he beat the Giants. The Phils shunted him to Cincinnati where he won only one game in 1910 and then disappeared into the minors. John McGraw had drummed him out of the league.

Why was Harry Coveleski so sensitive to the drumbeat?

It seems that McGraw found out that Harry had been courting a girl in Harry's hometown of Shamokin, Pennsylvania. Harry and his rival for the girl's hand both played in the school band—Harry played trumpet and his rival was the drummer. Coveleski's trumpet playing was so bad that the girl jilted him for the drummer. And Harry was never able to forget how the drummer had beaten him in the romantic duel.

The Tigers rescued Coveleski from the minors and he made a comeback in the American League. In his first three years with the Tigers, 1914–16, he won more than

20 games each season. Then his arm went dead and he drifted back to Shamokin.

But Harry Coveleski will be remembered in baseball as the pitcher who John McGraw drummed out of the league.

Everybody has fifteen minutes of fame . . . isn't that what Andy Warhol once said?

Saul Rogovin started his big-league career with the Tigers in 1949, and he hung around the majors through the 1957 season. I remember him best when he pitched for the Baltimore Orioles. He used to fall asleep on the bench. He had some type of sleeping sickness and sometimes just couldn't stay awake. He was intelligent and a hard worker, but never made his mark as a big leaguer—except for one game when he was with the Tigers.

It was Sunday, July 23, 1950. The Tigers were leading the league. They went into Yankee Stadium a half game ahead of the Yankees. Manager Red Rolfe picked Rogovin to start that big game. He faced the crafty Eddie Lopat.

Now, Saul Rogovin had grown up in Brooklyn, but he'd never been to Yankee Stadium—until this Sunday afternoon. It was a big occasion for him. All his family and friends were there. This was Saul's rookie year, and they'd never seen him pitch in the big leagues. Almost 60,000 fans were in the big park and Rogovin had knots in his stomach. He got by the first inning and then came his big moment—not on the mound, but at the plate.

Hoot Evers singled in the second inning. He moved to third on a double by Don Kolloway. Bob Swift was the next batter. Yankee manager Casey Stengel ordered Lopat to walk Swift to get to Rogovin. So, Saul stepped to the plate with the score tied, 0–0, and the bases loaded.

He choked up on the bat and dug in. Lopat served up

a slow curve and Rogovin swung. The ball shot off his bat
and kept going until it landed in the left-field seats. Over
his career, Saul hit only three home runs and his lifetime
batting average was .180, but for that one brief moment,
he was a grand-slam slugger.

Yes, Rogovin had his moment of glory, but many years
later he did something else you have to admire. After he
was out of baseball and more than 50 years old, Saul
decided to become a school teacher. He went to college
and graduated when he was 56. He is back in Brooklyn
now, teaching English at Eastern District High School.

And you can't blame Saul if once in a while he tells
those students about that Sunday afternoon when he hit
a grand slam at Yankee Stadium.

Nowadays, relief pitchers come in many varieties: the
short reliever, the long reliever and relievers for the relievers. But back in the 1920s, things were different.
Starting pitchers completed many more games and relievers weren't used as often.

There was one relief pitcher back then who was way
ahead of his time. He came into the game when the
starter was under fire—and no matter what inning it
was, he usually stayed in for the duration of the game to
win.

His name was William Wilcy Moore ... a right-
handed, somewhat awkward, good-natured country
bumpkin. He was born in Texas and grew up behind a
plow on an Oklahoma farm. He had the nerves of a New
York cabbie and the talent to make opposing batters
cringe. The first of many outstanding Yankee relievers,
he shared that ballclub's glorious season in 1927.

Moore began his career at the old age of 24 and spent
the first five years throwing primarily fastballs. But in
1925 he was hit by a batted ball, fracturing his pitching
arm. Because of that accident, he was forced to switch to

a sidearm sinker, and that was his ticket to the big leagues.

Word of his success in the minors reached Yankee general manager Ed Barrow. The plow hand had won 30 and lost 4 in 1926 at Greenville with an earned run average of 2.36. Late that season, Barrow sent a scout to check out Moore's abilities. The scout returned with news that the reliever said he was 30, but pitched like a 40-year-old.

Despite the unfavorable scouting reports, Moore signed with the Yankees early in 1927. He was joining the best pitching staff in baseball ... Hall of Famers like Waite Hoyt, Herb Pennock, Urban Shocker and Dutch Ruether.

By the middle of the season, the Yankee pitchers had finished 45 games; 40 of them were wins. But even these aces were human, and by the time the pennant was over, the 30-year-old rookie was 19 and 7. He played a key role in helping the Yankees win the World Series that year. He started, and completed, the final game of a four-game sweep, winning it 4–3.

All told, Moore appeared in 50 games in 1927. But he was a terrible hitter. Babe Ruth bet him $300 that he wouldn't get three hits all season. Moore won the bet, to the amazement of his Murderers' Row teammates. One hit was a home run right into Ruth's favorite target, the right-field stands. Moore bought two mules with the $300, which he fittingly named Babe and Ruth.

Unfortunately, Moore never again had a year as good as his rookie year with the Yanks, and he returned to the minors after several years of arm problems. In all, he played 13 of his 20 years in baseball in the minors.

A baseball manager's life is filled with misjudgments. Some are minor, but some are so major that they are never forgotten.

Casey Stengel always remembered a misjudgment he made in 1942.

Stengel was managing the Boston Braves. In a spring-training game against the Dodgers he wanted to take a look at a young pitcher named Warren Spahn, so he gave him the start.

As the game progressed, Stengel instructed Spahn to throw at the batter, Pee Wee Reese. But Spahn did not brush back Reese—he merely threw the ball inside. Two more times, Casey shouted instructions—each time, he got the same results.

When Spahn came to the bench, Stengel told him: "Young man, you've got no guts. I'm sending you to the Hartford club as soon as the game is over."

Casey recalled later, "Imagine that. I talked that way to a man who became a war hero and one of the best pitchers of all time."

Over the years Tiger manager Sparky Anderson has taken quite a ribbing about some of the statements he has made building up various players—Chris Pittaro, Barbaro Garbey and Torey Lovullo—just to name a few. Sparky understands and seems to be able to shake off the jibes.

But The Spark is not the only one who has gone wrong with an appraisal or two. The *Baseball Digest* looked into that situation a couple years ago and writer Glenn Liebman came up with some good examples.

In 1975 a young pitcher named John D'Acquisto was with the San Francisco Giants, and his manager—Wes Westrum—was waxing enthusiastic. Westrum said the newcomer had every bit as many pitching tools as Tom Seaver.

Well, he must have left them in his tool box. His final victory total was 277 less than Seavers' 311.

Then there was Ed Goodson. Padres manager Preston

Gomez said that this young San Francisco Giant slugger "had the batting champion's look about him." Somewhere along the way Goodson lost that look. He had only one decent year out of eight in the majors and ended up with a lifetime .260 average.

Along came Phil Ortega to the Dodgers. Dodger executive Fresco Thompson said he was going to be another Don Drysdale. His final win total was 46—163 fewer than Drysdale's 209.

It's been said that no modern player was a better student of hitting than Ted Williams. Yet, Ted tagged Lou Limmer as a great hitter. Lou's career batting average wasn't that great—he hit .202 and only played two years.

Sometimes it goes the other way. The expert doesn't recognize greatness and the prospect makes him eat his words.

Branch Rickey was an astute judge of talent. Yet, here's what Branch said about a young man named Yogi Berra: "The boy is too clumsy and slow. He's never going to be better than a triple-A ballplayer."

And here's Ted Williams again, this time with an appraisal of Roger Maris: "Maris is a dumpy little guy who reminds you of Mickey Mantle—but in build only."

Solly Hemus, the Cardinal manager, told Curt Flood: "You'll never make it." Flood became one of the best center fielders of his time and finished with a lifetime batting average just under .300.

A scout asked a rawboned rookie who had been wild why he didn't use the rosin bag. "Couldn't use it," the rookie said. "Couldn't get that knot untied on that little pouch."

Manager Earl Weaver once said: "The best place for a rookie pitcher is long relief. You can evaluate him without damaging his self-confidence."

Who was the last man to pitch to Babe Ruth? Jim Bivin, a rookie right-hander with the Phillies, retired Babe on that final at bat May 30, 1935 at Philadelphia.

FIVE

Adding Insult to Injury

"Some people give their bodies to science; I gave mine to baseball."

Ron Hunt

Sometimes in baseball you run across a star who was great, but for only a short time. I think one of the best examples is Joe Wood, who pitched for the Boston Red Sox. "Smoky Joe," they called him. He came to the Boston team from Kansas at the age of only 18. That was 1908. Three years later, he was one of the game's top pitchers, winning 23 games in 1911. And the next season, he was fabulous. He won 16 straight games—an American League record. At the age of only 22, he racked up 34 victories against only five losses and went on to pitch the Red Sox to three victories over the Giants in the World Series.

Talk about sitting on top of the baseball world! Joe Wood was there ... but it didn't last long. The next spring Wood broke his thumb trying to field a grounder. His hand was put in a cast and he was out of action. He came back too soon, and when he tried to pitch again he developed an ache in his shoulder. He pitched with great pain and managed to win only 11 games. He won only nine the following year and then struggled to a victory mark of 15 in 1915. But the arm just didn't respond, and Smoky Joe Wood knew that he was through.

So, at the age of 25 he went back home to Kansas. His career, a great one, was cut short because of injury. Still, Smoky Joe was different. He didn't like the idea of being out of baseball. He was restless and wanted to get back into action again.

His old Boston teammate Tris Speaker was now managing the Cleveland Indians. Joe got in touch with him and got another chance—as an outfielder. At the age of 27, Joe Wood was looked upon as a relic from another era, but he did the job. He played six seasons with the Indians, batting .366 once and playing outfield on the world champion Indians of 1920 when they whipped the Brooklyn Dodgers, 5 games to 2.

Smoky Joe with Cleveland never touched the heights he had reached with the Red Sox as a 34-game winning pitcher. But he did prove that you can come back.

What kind of a legend is this?

Here's a baseball player who has gone down in history as famous in two ways: A major-league team's nickname is derived from his exploits, and he was the inspiration for the famous fictional Frank Merriwell stories.

Yet, this so-called legend played only parts of three years in the major leagues. He appeared in less than 100 games and hit only three home runs.

His name: Louis Sockalexis.

The "Big Indian" was one of the truly tragic figures of baseball—a man with great talent and potential whose life was one of failure and sadness.

There's a lot of myth in the story of Sockalexis, but there are facts, too. Sockalexis was a Penobscot Indian. His grandfather had been a tribal chief. Louis was born in Maine and grew up there. Stories of his prowess abounded—even before he was out of high school. It was said that he had hit a home run more than 600 feet and could throw a baseball across the Penobscot River. One of the managers of an opposing team in the Maine summer leagues—Gilbert Patten—was so inspired by Sockalexis' play that he used him as the model for his popular Frank Merriwell stories—written under Patten's pen name of Burt L. Standish.

What had he done to gain such popularity? Louis Sockalexis was one of the baseball phenoms of the 19th century. After high school in Maine, he starred in baseball at Holy Cross and later Notre Dame. The Cleveland club signed him off the Notre Dame campus for $1,500, and he began his pro career with that big-league organization in 1897. He was an immediate sensation. His name was a constant headline and he packed the ballparks around the league.

In early July the Big Indian was hitting .328 with 39 runs batted in and 16 stolen bases. Then his world caved in. He was celebrating the night of July 4 with an all-night party. Drinking heavily, he fell from a second-story window and injured his ankle. Always a drinker, Sockalexis had trouble fighting off the urge while he was on the injured list. His idleness led to more indulgence and started his downfall. He played only once in August and twice in September.

Then came two more seasons in which he played very little for the Cleveland team—only 28 games and some of those as a pinch hitter. He was released and bounced around the minor leagues in New England, but never was able to stick with one team.

Finally, he retired to the Penobscot community and was working as a woodcutter when he died in 1913 at the age of 42. A Cleveland paper in 1915 conducted a contest to pick a nickname for the Cleveland team. The winning name was "Indians." The fan who submitted that name said he did so in honor of Sockalexis, the first American Indian to play in the big leagues.

In 1934, the State of Maine honored the Big Indian in a formal ceremony at his grave in the tribal cemetery. In '56, Holy Cross named him as the first inductee into its Athletic Hall of Fame.

An anonymous fan penned this poem during the season of 1897:

This is bounding Sockalexis, fielder of the mighty
    Cleveland.
Like a catapult in action, for the plate he throws the
    baseball,
'Til the rooter, blithely rooting, shouts until he
    shakes the bleachers.
Sockalexis, Sockalexis ...
Sock it to them, Sockalexis.

Sometimes it takes just a small push to propel a man from obscurity into the sports spotlight.

Not many even rabid fans knew much about Emil "Dutch" Levsen until several years ago when *Sport Magazine* came out with a quiz contest. One of the questions was: Which American League pitcher was the last to pitch and win two complete games in one day?

Enter Emil Levsen. Pitching and winning a double-header used to be fairly common. Joe "Iron Man" McGinnity won a nickname for such a feat when he did it in the early 1900s, but it's out of style now. No pitcher has accomplished the double-win since Levsen did it on August 28, 1926.

Levsen was a big blond German from Iowa—a man who entered baseball not by choice, but by necessity. He had studied farming at Iowa State College, then entered the business of cattle-raising with his brother. But the cattle business fell on hard times, and Levsen had to look elsewhere to survive. He turned to baseball, a sport he had played in college. After three years in the minors, he made the majors with Cleveland as a 26-year-old rookie.

Levsen's pitching feat on that August day was his sole claim to baseball fame. He beat the Boston Red Sox in the first game of the double-header, 5–1 and then volunteered to work the second. He won that one, 6–1.

All of this happened in his rookie year. He went on to win 17 games, but won only three more in later years. It was said that he pitched his arm out in winning the double-header, but Levsen says that isn't so, that he really hurt his arm in spring training the next season.

He is almost an unknown in the list of Tiger heroes, but his career was as brilliant as it was abbreviated. His name was Dale "Moose" Alexander, a big lumbering first baseman who was one of the game's great hitters.

Dale won the American League batting title in 1932, playing first with the Tigers and then the Red Sox. He is the only American League batting champion to be traded during a season. (Two National Leaguers also have that distinction: one was Harry "The Hat" Walker, who won the National League title in 1947 while playing for both the St. Louis Cards and the Philadelphia Phillies; the other was Willie McGee, whose .335 mark stood up after he was traded in August 1990 from the St. Louis Cardinals to the Oakland A's.)

Alexander won his batting title in a race against some fantastic hitters: Babe Ruth, Jimmie Foxx, Lou Gehrig, Charlie Gehringer and Al Simmons to name a few. He hit .367 that year, which was only his fourth season in the majors.

Dale was always a hitter. After a partial season in 1923

with Greenville in the Appalachian League, he began to blossom. With that same club the next year he batted .331. Then he moved to Charlotte and for the next two seasons compiled averages of .331 and .325. He moved up again in 1927—this time to Toronto. He batted .338 his first year there, and in 1928 jumped his average to .380 and hit 31 home runs.

The Tigers grabbed him and he broke in with a bang. He led the league in hits—215—in his rookie season of 1929. He played in 155 games and batted .343. He also set the American League record for most triples by a rookie (15), hit 25 homers, and knocked in 137 runs. The next two years he hit .326 and .325, then won the batting title in 1932 with an average of .367.

However, the next season—1933—was Alexander's last. He injured his leg while playing with the Red Sox. Treatment for the leg was inadequate and infection set in. His leg never recovered enough usefulness and he had to quit. With modern medical methods, that leg could have been saved and Alexander's career would have continued.

But it didn't happen that way. A great hitter was stopped by injury. Despite the poor '33 season, Alexander finished his five-year big-league career with a lifetime batting average of .331.

Why did the Tigers trade the big guy in mid-season, the year he won the batting title? Manager Bucky Harris was fed up with Dale's fielding lapses and the Tigers weren't going anywhere that year anyway. So Alexander and Roy Johnson were dealt to the Red Sox in exchange for Earl Webb.

Webb played only 87 games for the Tigers that year; and only six in 1933 before he was traded again, this time to the White Sox. Fifty-eight more games with them and his big-league career was over.

He had one of the best nicknames in recent Detroit Tigers history. He was emotional and he was colorful, but he didn't last long. His name was Kevin Saucier ... better known as "Hot Sauce." Hot Sauce and "Señor Smoke" (Aurelio Lopez) were a good one-two punch in the Tiger bullpen in the early 1980s. Lopez stayed around and made a real contribution, but Hot Sauce cooled off quickly.

Saucier signed right out of high school with the Phillies. He was in their bullpen in 1978, '79 and '80 and pitched in both the playoffs and the World Series. The Phils traded him to Texas. He never pitched there, but came to Detroit in exchange for Tiger shortstop Mark Wagner. In 1981 he had a 4 and 2 record and racked up 13 saves with a 1.65 ERA. All of a sudden he was a star and on a roll.

Saucier was an emotional performer and the Detroit fans loved his antics. After a win, he would bang his glove and jump high in the air. Even after he struck out a batter, it looked as if he would celebrate right then and there. He looked mean and aggressive, but down inside he was fighting to gain confidence.

He did fairly well in '82 and then his whole world collapsed. Eventually his emotions did him in. Almost overnight, he couldn't locate the plate. In mid-season of 1982 the Tigers had no choice but to send him back to the minors. He went to Evansville, but couldn't improve. The next spring at Lakeland, he was no better and the Tigers gave up. He landed with the Braves farm club in Richmond, but couldn't regain his control and finally drifted away from baseball. It was one of the few times I've seen a big-league pitcher unable to locate the plate with any of his pitches—partly due to a lack of confidence and partly to a mental block.

After baseball, Kevin went home to Pensacola—still less than 30 years old. He tried the pizza business, but without success. Then he turned to scouting, working for the major-league scouting bureau. Last I heard, he was still doing that.

It seems there are countless reasons why guys don't stick in the majors. Sam Byrd, of course, gave up baseball because he had become much more proficient at golf; and besides, Sammy decided—and wisely, too—that golf could last him a great deal longer than the diamond sport. George Sisler saw his career cut short by aggravating sinus trouble. Mark Koenig and Chick Hafey both were victims of eye weaknesses.

And what about Hal Peck? He was going up to the Brooklyn club until he shot off two of his toes while playing around with a shotgun.

Then, there was the Giant rookie who broke his ankle tripping over a loose bat. And thousands of would-be stars who couldn't be handled because they themselves couldn't handle that stuff that comes in a bottle—and I don't mean hair tonic.

Claude Rossman, one-time first baseman of the Detroit Tigers, had throwing trouble. Claude had a good strong arm, all right, but somehow, somewhere he began to think he couldn't throw. He developed a complex. Other American League clubs found out his weakness and after a while Rossman was back in the minors.

Then there's the story of George Susce—a player many insiders will remember because of nine honest words. Susce came to Detroit in the late stages of the 1934 Tiger pennant drive. At the time, the Tiger third baseman, Marvin Owen, was up to his ears in a fine batting streak. His hitting was great, and he was helping the Tigers immensely.

Now everybody on the club realized that Owen was hitting far over his head. They knew that he was an average hitter and no better than that—just a guy who would hardly ever bat .300.

Our friend Susce joined the Tigers on a Friday afternoon, but didn't play in that particular game. The next day—Saturday—he and Owen were sitting on the dugout steps.

"Say, Marv," Susce asked, "what ya hitting?"

Owen, quite proud of his average, was quick to answer, "Oh, I'm hitting .365."

Susce picked up a handful of dirt and tossed it away. There was not a trace of envy in his heart nor a bit of dishonesty in his soul.

He spoke. "You'll soon be down to .280 where you belong," he said candidly.

Mickey Cochrane, Tiger manager, overheard the remark . . . Cochrane, who so desperately was trying to keep up Owen's confidence, trying to keep him on his great hitting streak.

The next day George Susce was on his way to Milwaukee . . . with nine honest words he cut himself out of a share of the big dough of the World Series.

Owen's average? It did drop—but only to .317, his only .300 + year out of nine in the majors.

You have to go back more than 100 years, but the Tigers once had a pitcher with the unlikely nickname of "Lady." Not an attractive—or appropriate—nickname, especially in that rough and tough era when he pitched. That name of Lady belonged to Charles Baldwin, who survived with it for 11 years.

Most of Lady's fame—outside of his nickname—came from one fantastic season with the Detroit team of 1886. The Detroit team was not called the Tigers in those days, but the Wolverines. Lady Baldwin stood out in that one season of '86 by winning 42 games against 13 losses. He also captured four more victories in post-season competition, but that happened the next year when the Detroits met the St. Louis Browns in that early version of what we now call the World Series.

Baldwin's family moved from Ormel, New York to Hastings, Michigan when Charles was 18. A left-hander, he started as a pro with the Grand Rapids team in 1883 and then went to Milwaukee the next year. Milwaukee was in the Union Association, considered to be a major league. When he came to Detroit the next year, Baldwin was 26 and was reaching the height of his career.

After that one good year in 1886, he began to fade. So much, in fact, that in July of '87, the overworked pitcher was sent home to Hastings, without pay. Incidentally, his salary that year was considered to be a high one—$3,200 for the season.

Soon, his arm went dead, and Lady Baldwin was never effective again. He pitched three more seasons with Brooklyn, Buffalo, Binghamton and finally Grand Rapids, where in 1894 he finished his career in the same town he started it.

After his retirement, Baldwin went back to his farm in Hastings. Later he started a real estate business and was quite a success.

That nickname is still somewhat of a mystery. He was called Lady in an era when the players were rough and unsophisticated. He was not effeminate, but a rugged, athletic pitcher. The nickname probably came to him because he behaved himself the way ladies were supposed to behave: He didn't drink, smoke or swear, an unusual combination in those times.

From George Stallings to Sparky Anderson, Tiger managers have come and gone since 1901, the year Detroit became a part of the American League.

There should be one more name on that list of Tiger managers, but he never made it. Well, he did and he didn't. This man was selected to be a Tiger manager, but never did manage the team.

His name was Win Mercer. Win had pitched for the Tigers in 1902 under manager Frank Dwyer, but owner Samuel F. Angus moved Dwyer into the business office after the 1902 season and named a new manager for the upcoming 1903 season: pitcher Win Mercer. Win had spent most of his career with the Washington club—then in the National League. Twice he won more than 20 games for them. Then he went to the Giants, the Washington team in the American League, and, in 1902, won 15 games for Detroit.

Mercer was to manage the 1903 Tigers and also pitch for them. But in January of 1903 he killed himself in the Oriental Hotel in San Francisco. Mercer had traveled to the West Coast with a team of big-league all-stars. He had gambled and suffered big losses. He left letters of explanation to his mother and his fiancée, both of Liverpool, Ohio. He also wrote a letter to Tip O'Neill, who was in charge of the trip, and gave Tip a full statement of his accounts.

There's much mystery to the would-be manager's death. All we know today is that he had suffered with tuberculosis and was depressed and discouraged.

Mercer was a Tiger manager . . . but one who never got to see the team he would manage.

When Hank Greenberg was hurt in the 1935 World Series, Tiger owner Frank Navin told manager Mickey Cochrane to move Marv Owen to first and Flea Clifton to third. The Tiger players grumbled, but Navin took full responsibility, and the Tigers went on to win.

Joe Borden pitched a no-hitter in his debut for Philadelphia in 1875 and got a three-year contract at the unheard-of-price of $2,000. But his arm went bad, he never won again, and he had to work out his contract as a groundskeeper.

SIX

The Hits Just Keep on Coming

"All I can tell 'em is I pick a good one and sock it. I get back to the dugout and they ask me what it was I hit and I tell 'em I don't know except it looked good."

Babe Ruth

The best hitter I have ever seen is Ted Williams. Tall, rangy, graceful at the plate, he had great vision, concentration and coordination. He wasn't too interested in the fielding phase of baseball; hitting was his entire interest. He was always asking questions about various pitchers or other hitters. He talked to other players and old-timers about the science of hitting. He would even ask me and others in the media about certain new players or other players he had seen very little of. For the most part, Ted didn't care for the media. Lucky for me, I got along great with him. We had some long, interesting conversations. He has always been a man of great enthusiasm about his interests, very outspoken and always probing.

Once in Baltimore, while I was broadcasting there, the Orioles had a special night for Williams. It was a farewell salute to him for his final appearance as a player at Memorial Stadium. Ted impressed me that night by the thoroughness with which he approached the program. I was the emcee. Several hours before the game, he summoned me to the Red Sox clubhouse.

"Hey, I've got my speech ready," he said. "I wanted to ask you to take a look at it. See what you think."

I read the words he had written for himself on a piece of note paper. It was good, and I told him so. He thanked me and then went out and delivered it like a pro.

A lot of people don't remember that Williams' baseball records would have been even more remarkable except for the fact that he lost five playing years in two separate hitches with the Marine Air Corps. Yet, he still collected a total of 2,654 hits, banged out 521 home runs and is the only American Leaguer to win two Triple Crowns.

Ted's most publicized feat is probably his .406 batting average in 1941, the last man in baseball to hit over the .400 mark. He also had 37 home runs that season. He led the American League in hitting six times. His lifetime batting mark is the sixth best at .344. Williams was a shoo-in for the Hall of Fame. He was elected in 1966.

Ask around about Ted as a manager and you get different opinions. Most baseball people rank him no better than average. Maybe as a superstar he expected too much of his players. And there was a question, too, about how well he communicated with them.

I'll remember Ted as the most selective of hitters. Once in a game in Washington he was at bat against the Senators with a count of 2 and 2 on him. The Washington pitcher fired a pitch across the plate, Williams took it, figured he was out and started back to the bench. Umpire John Rice yelled at him, "Come back Ted, that was ball three." The Senators couldn't believe it. They knew Williams usually got a break on the strike zone from the umps, but this one was ridiculous. Ted returned to the plate and stroked a single to right on the next pitch.

"Why were you such a great hitter?" I asked Ted Williams recently.

"Well," he said, "where I lived as a kid had a lot to do with it. I lived in a good climate—San Diego—and I lived only a block or so from my grammar school. I was over there every morning before the janitor got there. As soon as he arrived, I went to the closet, got out a ball and bat and began to practice hitting."

Ted said he hit whenever he could—even under the lights at nighttime—practicing and studying the art.

"One day," he said, "some adult on the playground looked at me and said: 'That kid sure has great wrists.' That made me feel terrific . . . just that offhand remark. But I said to myself, 'Mr., you think those wrists are great now, just wait a year or two.'"

Ted worked out as a youngster with the San Diego team, and even before he signed was taking a lot of batting practice. There he ran into Lefty O'Doul, who told him something that had a profound effect on the young Mr. Williams. Ted went to O'Doul for hitting advice. They sat down on the grass out in the right-field corner.

"Mr. O'Doul," Ted asked the veteran, "what do I have to do to be a big-league hitter?"

Lefty put his hand on Ted's shoulder and said, "Kid, just one thing: Don't let anybody ever try to change the way you hit."

I asked Ted the obvious question: "In your whole career, did anybody ever try to change you?"

"That's funny," he said. "Really only one guy did, and you won't believe who it was. Of all the great hitters and coaches I ever talked to about hitting, only one player ever suggested any changes—a Red Sox pitcher named Joe Dobson. Dobson knew absolutely nothing about hitting, but he would always call me aside and say 'do this and do that.' I never paid any attention to him. What he told me went in one ear and out the other."

Williams did make one small adjustment in his hitting. When the opposition began to pull the famous Williams shift on him and played him completely around to right field, he adjusted. Pittsburgh great Paul Waner suggested it to Williams, telling him to step back a foot from the plate, so he would let a level, inside-out swing hit the ball to left field. Ted followed the advice and the maneuver proved successful for him.

Williams' greatest thrill? His answer surprised me. It wasn't hitting .406, or his final home run at Fenway. No, he said his biggest thrill was his game-winning home run with two out in the ninth at Detroit in the 1941 All-Star Game.

"I was only 22 at the time," he said. "It gave me a bigger kick than anything else I've ever done."

The game's super hitter—that was Ted Williams.

Baseball people are always talking about records that will never be broken ... Joe DiMaggio's 56-game hitting streak and Johnny Vander Meer's two consecutive no-hitters, just to name a couple. But you never hear much about another record that should be just about unbreakable.

How about 257 hits in one season? St. Louis Browns first baseman George Sisler set that one in 1920. Two National Leaguers came close: Lefty O'Doul had 254 hits for the Phillies in 1929, and the next year Bill Terry of the Giants also had 254.

But since then, nobody has threatened the mark. In 1985 Wade Boggs of the Red Sox had his greatest year, compiling 240 hits. He played in 161 games that season and batted 653 times. His hit total was the highest in the majors since Terry's 254 in 1930.

But compare Boggs' 240 hits to Sisler's 257. Sisler played in all his team's 154 games and batted 631 times—22 less at bats than Boggs.

Sisler's hit total was not his only achievement that year. What a season he turned in. He won the National League batting title with a .407 average, was first or second in doubles, triples, home runs, runs batted in, runs scored, total bases, slugging percentage and stolen bases. Not bad, and what's more, he struck out only 19 times in those 631 times at bat.

Sisler went hitless in only 30 games. Only twice did he go as many as two straight games without a hit. And there were only two pitchers who held him hitless twice while pitching complete games.

Five players in this century have hit higher than Sisler's .407 mark in 1920—including Sisler himself who batted .420 in 1922—but none of those batting stars collected more than 248 hits. (Joe Jackson hit .408 in 1911; Ty Cobb hit .410 in 1912 and .420 in 1911; Nap Lajoie hit .422 in 1901; and Rogers Hornsby hit .424 in 1924.)

Sisler was a great fielder, too. Many think he was the best ever at his position. He started out as a pitcher and was a graduate of the University of Michigan. Branch Rickey once said he thought Sisler was the greatest player he had ever seen.

Bad health cut his career short. After he batted .420 in 1922, Sisler sat out the entire 1923 season. Inflammation of the sinus had affected his optic nerves and had given him double vision. He came back in 1924 as player-manager of the Browns and despite his vision problems, he still hit over .300 and had several good years left.

Sisler retired with a lifetime batting average of .340 and will always be ranked as one of baseball's greats, and his one-season mark of 257 hits stands a high and distant target.

It always pays to hustle ... that's an adage as old as baseball itself. Back in 1930, Lefty O'Doul felt the bite of that old saw when lack of hustle cost him the ownership of an all-time National League record.

The previous year, 1929, O'Doul had won the National League batting title. In doing so he had collected the most hits in the history of the league—254. Then along came 1930 and Bill Terry. Terry won the batting title in 1930 and also collected 254 hits to tie O'Doul's record.

But Terry tied O'Doul for one reason only: O'Doul's lack of hustle on one play. New York's Terry lifted a foul fly off first base, Philadelphia's O'Doul didn't chase it far enough, and the fly fell safely into foul territory. Given another chance, Terry then lined a single to right. It was his final hit of the 1930 season and number 254 to tie O'Doul's record.

From then on, until the end of his career, Lefty O'Doul hustled on every play.

Down through the years of baseball history, there have been many home-run heroes—great names who made the headlines scream with their long wallops. The top three would have to be Babe Ruth, Roger Maris and Hank Aaron. Ruth, the first big home-run record setter, changed the game with his 60 home runs in one season. Along came Maris and broke the record. And more recently, Hank Aaron surpassed Ruth's all-time career record for home runs.

But what about Joe Bauman? Yes, Joe Bauman. He hit a total of 72 home runs in one season. Ruth's one-season record was 60, Maris beat that by one, but Bauman hit 72.

He didn't do it in the big leagues, but he still did it, and that was quite a feat.

Joe Bauman was a 6'5," 235-pound left-handed hitter.

He played for Roswell, New Mexico in the old Class C
Longhorn League. In his super year of 1954, Joe Bauman
hit a home run in every 6.9 times at bat. He led the
league with a .400 batting average. He had 225 runs batted in. Bauman also walked 150 times and played in
every one of his team's 183 games. His slugging percentage was .916—69 points better than the best of Babe
Ruth.

But Joe never played in the majors. He did appear in
one game for Milwaukee in Triple A. But other than that,
he never played in a league higher than Class A.

Just a journeyman ballplayer, Joe even quit the pro
ranks after 1948 and played semi-pro ball for three seasons. When he set his home-run record in 1954 at
Roswell, he also owned a gas station there. When the
Roswell Rockets were home, Joe pumped gas in the day-
time and hit home runs at night.

What about the park that Bauman hit in at home? It
was nothing extraordinary. His target, the right-field
fence, was 10 feet high and 329 feet from home plate.

When Bauman hit his 72 homers, he didn't even get a
raise. The next season he slumped to 46 home runs and
132 RBI. In '56, injuries struck him down and he quit in
mid-season, after hitting 17 home runs in 52 games.

In Tiger history you can designate your heroes by eras:
In the early 1900s it was Sam Crawford, then Ty Cobb;
later came Harry Heilmann; then Charlie Gehringer and
Mickey Cochrane. Along with them came the great Hank
Greenberg; after Hank, it was Hal Newhouser, George
Kell, Al Kaline and Denny McLain. Now we have Alan
Trammell and Cecil Fielder.

But there was none more heroic in his time than Hank
Greenberg. Many a Detroit Jewish kid went to sleep on
a summer night with his glove under his pillow and
dreams that someday he would be another Hank Green-

berg. Henry is Detroit's number one home-run man. In his Tiger lifetime, Kaline hit more homers; but Greenberg hit 58 in 1938, an all-time Tiger high for one season. That was the year he almost beat Babe Ruth's record.

No man ever worked harder at his craft than Hank Greenberg. A season that epitomized Greenberg's diligence was 1940. It was the season he won the MVP award for the second time. He switched that year—as a gesture of team spirit—from first base to outfield. He worked hard to become an outfielder. And despite breaking into a strange position, Hank hit .340, drove in 150 runs and hit 41 home runs.

Greenberg went into the Army during the next season and gave up four years of his big-league career to the war effort. When he returned to the Tigers at the end of the '45 season, he hit a dramatic ninth-inning bases-loaded home run to give the Tigers the pennant.

1946 was his final year in Detroit. He was back at first base, and he led the league in home runs and runs batted in. After that, Greenberg was sold to Pittsburgh and finished his career there in 1947.

But to all of baseball he always seemed to belong to Detroit. He was the genuine hero of the Tigers in the '30s and '40s—not only a great star, but a classy gentleman who fitted the true mold of a hero.

Charlie "King Kong" Keller was named after the star of the movie of the same name—that big gorilla that knocked over New York skyscrapers. Keller was a big guy, but very gentle—until he grabbed a baseball bat. Keller was a great hitter from the start of his career.

His first year in baseball was at Newark. He batted .353 and knocked in 88 runs. He was named the _Sporting News_ minor-league player of the year. In his first Yankee season, 1939, he hit .334 and was the hero of the World Series as the Yankees swept past Cincinnati in four straight. Charlie batted .438 in that Series, scoring eight runs and driving in six in the four games. It was quite a World Series for a boy only out of college less than three years.

Keller stayed with the Yankees through 1949. He was one of their big stars: In three seasons he knocked in more than 100 runs; three times his home-run total went over the 30 mark.

The Yanks released Keller in December 1949, and he signed with the Tigers. During the 1950 season, Charlie helped the Tigers in their bid for the pennant. He played in 50 games and batted .314. He stayed on for the 1951 season and then returned to the Yanks in 1952. Always troubled by an ailing back, Keller finally called it quits after a couple games and went back to the farm in Maryland to raise horses.

When Charlie would dig in at the plate in his prime, somebody from that other dugout would always yell, "Hey, Keller, did they sign you or trap you?" That was King Kong Keller, a slugger in the true Yankee tradition.

During his broadcasting career, Harry Heilmann was modest about his baseball stardom and always referred to his playing days with warm, good humor. But the real baseball fan knew all about Harry. For 17 years he was one of the best who ever put on a Tiger uniform. He won four American League batting titles and won his way to the Hall of Fame with a lifetime hitting mark of .342. That lifetime average would be good enough to win a championship in most American League seasons now.

In his first three years with the Tigers—1916, '17 and '18—he didn't reach the .300 mark. But then, with instructions from his manager, Ty Cobb, he came on strong—so strong that when he won his first batting title in 1921, he beat out the great Cobb himself. Heilmann

hit .394 that season. From then on, he was to win a batting championship every other year. And he won with
these averages: .403 in 1923, .393 in 1925, and .398 in
1927. He took a lot of kidding about his off-years when
he didn't take the championship. But any slugger these
days would settle for one of those Heilmann off-years:
.356, .346, .367 and .328.

A hitter like that had to be good, but the story which
epitomizes what a great clutch hitter Heilmann was is
the story of how he won the batting title in 1927—the
last one he captured. As the final day of the season arrived, Al Simmons of Philadelphia was leading Harry
by two points. The A's had one game that day; the Tigers
were scheduled for a double-header.

The A's were at Washington; the Tigers were playing
in Cleveland. Because of the time difference, Simmons
would begin and finish his day before Heilmann. Harry
hit a double in each of his first two trips. Now, word came
to the press box that the A's-Washington game was over
and that Simmons had two hits in five at bats to finish
at .392. Heilmann picked up a hit in his next two trips.
The press box sent him word that he now had passed
Simmons and the batting title was his.

But Harry Heilmann wouldn't quit and win the title
sitting it out. He came up again and hit a home run. He
even played the second game, putting his chance for the
title in jeopardy. And in that second game, he collected a
single, double and a home run in four times at bat. He
had beaten Simmons by six points.

True to his nature, Heilmann did it the hard way—not
sitting tight when he knew he had the championship
won, but going all out, playing that second game and
winning like a true champion.

Canada has given the big leagues many stars. The first
Canadian to play in the big leagues was William B. Phil-

lips, from St. John. He played first base and broke in with the Cleveland Club in the National League in 1879. Ten years later, he finished his career with Kansas City.

But Canada sent to the majors an even more vigorous hitter in the 19th century—a man whose record still stands as the best of any from that country. In fact, one of his marks has never been approached by any player, from anywhere.

He was James E. (Tip) O'Neill. Tip hailed from Woodstock and started as a pitcher with the New York Giants and then the St. Louis Browns. While with the Browns, he turned outfielder. In 1887, he played 124 games for the Browns and batted .435.

That happened to be the year that walks were scored as hits, but you still can't take it away from Tip. He did bat a magnificent .435.

In major-league baseball history, only 14 players have won the Triple Crown. And the last five have been American Leaguers: Carl Yastrzemski, Frank Robinson, Mickey Mantle and Ted Williams, who won it twice.

Rogers Hornsby of the Cards is the only star besides Williams to take the Triple Crown twice. The strangest record among Triple-Crown winners belongs to Ty Cobb, who took the honor in 1909. That year his league-leading home-run total was only nine. He also stole 76 bases that year.

Pete Rose eclipsed the 4,000-hit mark in 1984 amid intense media hoopla. Rose finished his career in 1986 with a major-league record 4,256. But the only other man to get 4,000 hits, Ty Cobb, collected his No. 4,000 almost in private. There was no television then, almost no radio and the Detroit papers practically ignored the historic event.

It happened in 1927. On July 18, Cobb had returned to Detroit's Navin Field as a member of the Philadelphia Athletics. Cobb's 4,000th—a double—came in the first inning against his old team, the Tigers.

In the *Detroit Free Press,* Cobb's hit didn't even make a headline, nor the lead paragraph of the game story. After four paragraphs, the hit got a bare mention. In a column of notes, there was a mention, but it came in the fifth paragraph, after the writer had listed the Tiger schedule and the fact that the home team didn't make a double play in the game.

In the entire sports section there was no photo of Cobb, no stats, or any other notice of the hit.

The *Detroit News* did note Cobb's hit in a headline—a headline equal in size to one about a Detroit team winning the YMCA basketball title. The game story had one sentence on the Cobb two-bagger. And the great H. G. Salsinger, who covered the Tigers, wrote a column that day, but it was not about Cobb. It concerned pro boxing.

The *News*—like the *Free Press*—had no photo, no special story on the hit—nothing.

Apparently people didn't make a big to-do about such events back then. The game wasn't stopped, nor was the ball given to Cobb. The fans didn't cheer for him to come from the dugout to take a bow. And certainly, the reports just about ignored the historic moment. Times do change, don't they?

Ty Cobb was the fiery genius of baseball. No player could match his competitive dash and his studied skill. He was so good that as the years go by, he becomes even more incredible. In his 24 years in the American League, he led the league in batting 12 times—nine of those years coming in succession. His lifetime batting average was .367.

Ty's arm was strong and his feet were fast. On the bases he was the best. He stole a total of 892 bases in his career. But more than that, he was always a threat. Pitchers became as nervous as colts when Ty took a lead off the bag. All the fielders would become jittery in the fear that he might take an extra base.

So feared was Ty as a base stealer that manager Connie Mack of the Athletics once posed this question to his catcher, Wally Schang: "Now suppose Cobb was on second and you knew he was going to steal third. What would you do?"

Schang shot back this answer: "That's easy. I'd call for a pitchout, fake a throw to third, hold onto the ball and try to tag him as he slid home."

For a very long time now people in baseball have referred to any little pop fly dropping safely behind the infield as a "Texas Leaguer." But why?

Well, it goes back to a man named Arthur Sunday. Sunday was an outfielder from Springfield, Ohio. In the season of 1889 he was playing outfield under manager John McCloskey at Houston in the Texas League. Before the scheduled ending of the season, however, the Texas League folded.

Arthur Sunday left Texas and landed with the Toledo club in the International League. He played 31 games there and hit a cool .398. Most of his hits were little bloopers, just over the infield. Since Mr. Sunday had just come up from the Texas League, some writer called these hits "Texas Leaguers," and the term has been with us ever since.

If a young man wants fame and fortune in the game, the prime method to obtain it is home-run hitting.

And yet, at one time, the home run was almost sneered at.

Let's open up the *Reach Baseball Guide* for 1896 and

read some of the stilted prose of that era. The subject of this piece in the guide is Sam Thompson, one-time Detroit slugger. Here's the way it reads: "Thompson belongs to that rutting class of slugging batsmen who think of nothing else when they go to the bat but that of gaining the applause of the groundlings (the 1896 word for fans) by the novice's hit to the outfield of a homer, one of the least difficult hits known to batting in baseball, as it needs only muscle and not brains to make it."

It's the only time I've seen the lofty home run denigrated in print . . . but there it is.

This all points us to Mr. Thompson, who was certainly the early day home-run hitter. Sam Thompson was elected to the Baseball Hall of Fame in 1974. He is one of the two Detroit players named from the era when the Detroits were members of the National League. He batted .404 in 1894 and he still maintains the best ratio of runs-batted-in to games of any hitter in the history of baseball—and that includes Babe Ruth, Joe DiMaggio, Lou Gehrig, Hank Greenberg, or anyone else you want to name.

Sam—one of six brothers—intended to be a carpenter. He was repairing a roof back home in Indiana one 1883 afternoon when the Detroit team came through town for an exhibition. The folks of Danville wanted Sam to play against the big leaguers. He said okay, but you have to pay me more than I'm making repairing this roof. Sam got $2.50 to play that afternoon and forgot all about hammers and nails. He signed a contract with Evansville and two years later, at the age of 25, made it to the big leagues with Detroit.

Despite a late start, Thompson played 10 seasons in the National League and parts of five others. He was with two teams —Detroit and Philadelphia. His career batting average was .331 and he was credited with 128 home runs—the most by any National Leaguer until Rogers Hornsby came along.

Sam's high in homers any one season was 20. He accomplished that in 1889, and at that time 20 was a gigantic number for home runs in a season.

Thompson was regarded as a fine outfielder, with a good arm. He was not slow for a big man and twice stole 29 bases.

After Thompson's playing career was over, he lived in Detroit. He became a federal marshall and then court bailiff in the city. Every opening day when the mayor would toss out the first ball to Charley Bennett, Sam Thompson would serve as the honorary umpire.

Sam died in Detroit in 1922 at the age of 62. His widow refused to sell his home-run bat to a collector. By that time, the once-lowly home run had been elevated to its present status of dignity and esteem.

With a small break or two or another twist of luck, Jimmie Foxx might have broken Babe Ruth's home-run record for one season, long before Roger Maris arrived on the scene.

In 1932, Foxx hit 58 homers, but twice he hit home runs in early innings of games that were rained out. Three other times he hit balls against screens in St. Louis and Cleveland—screens that weren't in place when Ruth was having his greatest season.

In 1933, Foxx hit only 48 home runs, 10 less than the year before. He batted .356 and the A's tried to cut his salary from $16,333 to $11,000.

Foxx was versatile. He played infield, outfield, pitched and caught. His lifetime average was .325 and he hit a total of 534 home runs.

Frank "Home Run" Baker introduced Foxx to baseball. Baker managed Jimmy at Easton, Maryland in the Eastern Shore League in his first year—1924.

Baker offered Foxx to the New York Yankees, but Miller Huggins, the New York manager, showed no interest. So Baker handed Foxx over to Connie Mack and the Philadelphia A's.

The Yankees were devastating enough, but just suppose they had added Foxx to their power-laden lineup, which featured Ruth and Gehrig.

Foxx was as muscular as any hitter in history. He once took a fresh baseball out of the box and twisted the cover loose. And with the bat in his hands, he could often—as everybody said—tear the cover off the ball.

You can have the famous home runs of baseball: I'll take the crazy ones. You can have the hits that made headlines; I'll take those funny little blows that brought a chuckle and then were lost in the limbo of forgotten box scores.

Sure, it was great to see Dusty Rhodes' clouts in the World Series. It was wonderful to watch Babe Ruth, Home Run Baker, Dick Sisler and Bob Thomson swing and make history. But I'll settle for those home runs that traveled only two feet, went through holes in the fence, rolled up walls and made everybody laugh.

Of course, none will be quite like the one hit about 75 years ago by Grover Land, catcher for Brooklyn in the old Federal League. With Brooklyn playing at Chicago, umpire Barry McCormick didn't show up. So umpire Bill Brennen had to oversee the action —alone—from behind the pitcher's mound. Bill arranged his supply of extra baseballs near the mound in a neat pyramid.

Land came to bat and hit a line drive at the pile of baseballs, scattering them in all directions. Every infielder came up with one. Grove kept running, even though Chicago players tagged him at each base. When he crossed the plate, Brennen called him safe because nobody knew who had the right ball.

Though Land's home run didn't get past the infield, it was a long-distance clout compared to a homer hit 'way back by Andy Oyler of Minneapolis.

Rain had fallen all that day and the diamond was mushy. Oyler, a shortstop, sloshed his way to the batter's box. The St. Paul pitcher threw. In came the pitch straight at Oyler's head. He ducked. The ball hit his bat, spun away—and vanished.

The St. Paul first baseman looked under the bag. No baseball. The catcher scanned the sky. Nothing came down. Even the umpire was bewildered. Meanwhile, Oyler was slipping and sliding around the bases.

"He's got the ball in his pocket!" somebody yelled. When the St. Paul shortstop heard this, he began to follow Oyler around the bases.

"Watcha doin'?" he shouted as Oyler crossed the plate. "Gimme that ball!"

"I ain't got it," said Oyler. "It's right there in front of the plate."

And it was. The ball was buried in the mud—only two feet in front of the plate. A home run.

Many crazy things have happened in Brooklyn, but none crazier than the homer hit there by George Cutshaw in 1916. Cutshaw tapped what should have been an ordinary single to right field. The ball rolled to the bottom of the concave wall. It hit the bottom of the wall and climbed upwards. It reached the top, teetered, then dropped over the wall for a game-winning homer.

Another freakish four-bagger happened in the Pacific Coast League. Larry McLean smacked a drive which went through the only knothole in a short right field fence.

One of Babe Ruth's most interesting home runs was not an extra-long one—but it packed terrific force. He hit the ball so hard that it went through the pitcher's legs and on past the center fielder.

The day it happened, Hod Lisenbee was pitching for

Washington. Tris Speaker, center fielder for the Senators, crept in toward second in an attempt to trap a runner off base. As he did, Lisenbee pitched. The Babe smashed the ball right back through the box. The drive hit over second, struck a pebble and bounded high over Speaker's head. Ruth rounded the bases without interference.

Fans who saw that home run still talk about it. However, the one that really makes old-timers chuckle was hit by an early-day baseball clown named Herman (Germany) Schaefer, who played for Detroit. That day the Tigers were behind, 2–1, to the White Sox in the ninth. Schaefer was on the bench, recovering from an injury. Detroit manager Bill Armour turned to him.

"Feel good enough to hit for the pitcher?" he asked.

"Sure," Schaefer replied.

He then stalked to the plate, removed his cap, bowed and announced: "Ladies and gents, permit me to present Herman Schaefer, the world's premier batsman, who will give a demonstration of his marvelous hitting prowess. He will hit a home run into the left-field stands and win this game. I thank you."

Boos cascaded from the stands. Schaefer merely smiled and took his stance. He swung at the second pitch, and— true to his prediction—hit it into the left-field seats.

Herman sprinted to first base and slid into the bag. He hopped up and shouted: "The Great Schaefer leading at the quarter."

He slid into second and yelled: "The Great Schaefer in front at the half."

He slid into third and announced: "The Great Schaefer by five lengths at the three-quarters."

With extra speed he ran home and slid across the plate. Then he got up, carefully dusted off his dirty uniform and doffed his cap.

"This, ladies and gents," he announced, "concludes the afternoon performance. I thank you one and all."

Every Detroit Tigers fan has his own magic moment. For me there is one special moment frozen in the time frame of my mind. It was a moment that epitomizes the Tiger team and the Tiger season of 1984. My special, magic moment happened at Tiger Stadium on June 4 before a national television audience.

The Toronto Blue Jays had pulled within $4^1/2$ games of the league-leading Tigers. This Monday night game was the first meeting between the two top rivals in the Eastern Division. They battled through nine tense, tough innings and were tied, 3–3, in the last of the tenth.

There were two out. Tiger catcher Lance Parrish was on second and outfielder Chet Lemon on first. Now came the moment, a moment that reduced baseball to its simplest dimension: pitcher against batter.

It was Roy Lee Jackson, Toronto pitcher, against Dave Bergman, Tiger batter.

With two strikes on him, Bergman fouled off seven pitches. Then he smashed a 3–2 pitch into the right-field upper deck and the Tigers had won, 6–3.

Tiger coach Dick Traczewski put the Bergman heroics in perspective for all of us. As a player and coach, Traczewski has seen battles between pitchers and hitters for 30 years.

"It's the biggest single at-bat performance I've ever seen," Dick said in the Tiger clubhouse after the game. Manager Sparky Anderson agreed. All the Tigers were amazed at both the intensity and concentration Bergman showed in his one-on-one battle with Roy Lee Jackson.

To me, it was a symbol of the season.

Bergman was not a superstar. He was a player who came along as extra baggage in the Willie Hernandez deal. He was a hard-nosed, dedicated professional. He was a role player. He did not play every day, but was always ready when his manager needed him. Dave was hurt twice during the season. Yet, he never complained.

Bergman missed games in June (right after his heroic homer) because of a groin pull. In September he was out of action again with a sprained back. When he returned, there was a sense of *déja vu*. He was facing Toronto again—this time in Toronto. He banged out four hits against Blue Jay pitching. His final hit was another three-run home run—again in the tenth inning—which gave the Tigers a 7–4 win. That victory put the Detroiters $9^{1}/2$ games ahead of the Jays and settled the Eastern Division race.

It was a reprise of my magic moment: Dave Bergman at the plate against Roy Lee Jackson, June 4. Bergman fouls off seven pitches and then hits the game-winning home run. To me, that was 1984.

When Roger Maris hit 61 home runs in 1961, he did not receive a single intentional pass. Mickey Mantle batted behind him.

The all-time professional runs-batted-in leader was Bob Crues, who played for Amarillo. In 1948 Crues batted in 254 runs in 140 games. He hit .404, scored 185 runs and had 69 homers.

In 1927, Babe Ruth hit more home runs than any American League *team* except his own—the Yankees. His teammates hit 98 home runs that season; the Babe hit his longtime record 60. The Philadelphia Athletics hit 56; the Browns hit 55; the Tigers hit 51; the White Sox 36; the Senators 29; the Red Sox 28; and the Indians 26.

The old American League record for the most hits by a switch hitter in a season was held by Buck Weaver of

Chicago. He had 210 hits in 1920. The major-league record was set by Pete Rose in 1973, with 230. Then Willie Wilson of Kansas City hit 230 for the American League record in 1980. Incidently, Buck Weaver became a switch hitter in mid-season, and he didn't switch depending on right- or left-hand pitchers, but batted left-handed for accuracy and right-handed for power.

When the Yankees' Lou Gehrig was batting, the Tigers put five men on the right-field side of second base: Jack Burns, Charlie Gehringer, Billy Rogell and Gee Walker when he was playing center field and Pete Fox when he was playing right. Shortstop Rogell took a position on the grass about three feet to the right-field side of the bag. Gehringer moved over towards first.

When Babe Ruth was active, a ball hit out of the ballpark that then curved foul was ruled a foul ball. Since 1931, the rule says the judgment is made on where the ball crosses the foul line. Some say the Babe would have had a lot more home runs under the new rule.

Stan Musial might be described as a model of consistency. He had 3,630 career hits over 22 years—exactly half of them, 1,815, came on the road and the other half in St. Louis.

The heaviest bat ever ordered was 52 ounces by Babe Ruth. The heaviest ever used regularly was 48 ounces by both Ruth and Edd Roush, who played for the Reds; the lightest, 29 ounces, by Billy Goodman. The longest bat regularly used was 38 inches by Al Simmons; and the shortest, $30^{1}/_{2}$ inches by Wee Willie Keeler.

Catcher Lee Head of Knoxville in the Southern League struck out once in 402 times at bat in 1935. He never went to the big leagues. Joe Sewell of the Indians holds the major-league record: only four strikeouts in 608 at-bats in 1925.

The only player to lead each major league in home runs was Sam Crawford. He hit 16 for Cincinnati in 1901 and led the American League in 1908 when he hit seven for Detroit.

SEVEN

Throwing Smoke

"The space between the white lines—that's my office. That's where I conduct my business."

Early Wynn

The farm boy who was named for a cyclone—Cy Young—kept that nickname throughout his baseball career—a career that was the most productive of any pitcher in the history of the game. Young pitched for 22 years, won more games than any other pitcher (511), started a total of 815 regular season games and finished all but 65 of them.

It didn't take Cy long to make the big time. After he had signed with Canton, he moved on to Cleveland in 1890. He pitched his first game against the Chicago Colts. He won that game, 3–1, and allowed the Colts only three hits. He even fanned the famous Colt manager and slugger Pop Anson. Anson offered Cleveland $2,000 for their new pitcher, but was refused.

So, Cy had gained his first of 511 victories. And the

youngster who was to become the winningest of all hurl-
ers, was making exactly $75 a month.

Blazing speed and near-perfect control made Young
baseball's top pitcher. In five different seasons he won
more than 30 games. Fifteen times he bested the 20-mark
in victories. He pitched three no-hitters: one of those was
a perfect game against the Philadelphia Athletics on
May 5, 1904.

Young was 36 years old when he finally pitched in a
World Series. On the mound for the Red Sox, he bested
the Pittsburgh Pirates twice and lost to them once in the
1903 classic, the first of modern history. But the big right-
hander was still going strong in his mid-forties. It was
not until 1911 that he finally called it quits.

Before Young had retired, a signal honor came to him.
He became the only player in big-league annals to receive an award from all the players in his league.
Throughout the American League, players made dona-
tions to purchase a loving cup for Cy. It was inscribed:
"From the ballplayers of the American League, to show
their appreciation of Cy Young, as a man and as a ballplayer."

In 43 years of broadcasting in the big leagues, I've seen
seven no-hitters. And the no-hitter that Nolan Ryan
pitched against the Tigers on July 15, 1973 has to be tops.

Very close to that one would be the near-perfect game
pitched by Milt Wilcox against the White Sox at Comiskey Park on April 15, 1983. Milt was perfect until, with
two out in the ninth, Jerry Hairston hit the first pitch—a
line shot through the box for Chicago's only hit of the
game.

Wilcox turned in an outstanding performance, but the
one in 1973 by Nolan Ryan was even more remarkable. I
have never seen any pitcher as overpowering as Ryan
was for California that afternoon at Tiger Stadium.

You've heard the old expression: "They were lucky to hit a foul off him." Well, that was certainly true that afternoon.

It was Ryan's second no-hitter of that season. He struck out 17 and beat the Tigers easily, 6–0. His fastball was rising about six inches as it neared the plate, but the pitch that set him up was a slow curve. He had great control of that pitch and it showed a tremendous break.

You knew early in the game that it was going to be Ryan's day. He struck out 12 of the first 17 Tiger batters. His strikeouts had been so impressive that I was really concentrating more on his strikeout record than the fact that Nolan was pitching a no-hitter.

Jim Perry was pitching for the Tigers, and the game was close most of the way. After seven innings the Angels held on to a 1–0 lead. They had scored in the third on a sacrifice fly by Vada Pinson.

In the eighth, the Angels began to bang Perry around. Manager Billy Martin replaced Jim with Fred Scherman. Before the long half-inning was over, California had scored five runs. But the long inning took its toll on Ryan. The delay seemed to hurt him, and he lost his strikeout pitch. Still, he finished with a total of 17 strikeouts.

This was the game—celebrated in Tiger legend—in which Norman Cash came to bat and was sent back to the dugout because his bat was illegal. Cash told me later, "I wasn't gonna hit the guy anyway, so I went up to the plate with a leg off the table in the clubhouse."

Norman knew he was overmatched that day. His teammates were, too. Only three Tigers were able to get the ball out of the infield. And the Angel fielders had only one tough chance: Gates Brown hit a line drive in the ninth toward short, but Rudi Meoli leaped and grabbed it.

Ryan walked four and fanned every Tiger at least once. Dick McAuliffe and Duke Sims struck out three times apiece.

Ryan has six no-hitters now—a major-league record. But the one he spun July 15, 1973, was by far the best game I've ever seen anybody pitch.

There was a time in New York when Babe Ruth walked in from the outfield and took over on the pitching mound to strike out the great Ty Cobb. Cobb was manager of the Tigers then. Babe had not pitched for many years. The Yanks had a big lead. When Cobb came to bat in the seventh inning, Ruth came in to pitch.

"So," he yelled at Cobb, "you think you're a hitter, hey? You so-and-so, I haven't pitched in years, but I can still make you look like a busher."

Cobb blew a fuse—it was the only time in his 24-year career that he ever forgot what to do on the diamond. Cobb wanted a fastball. Ruth kept feeding him slow ones. Cobb was so outraged that he was swinging desperately to hit the ball out of the park ... and struck out.

Ruth trotted back to his position in the outfield. Cobb just stood at the plate, wanting to fight.

That was the Babe. A big guy with a flair for the dramatic. The one greatest hero of sports.

One of the strangest of all major-league pitching records belongs to a Tiger—Virgil Trucks. In 1952 Trucks had a record of five wins and 19 losses, but he pitched two no-hitters and barely missed a third.

It was a terrible season for the Tigers—the worst in their history. They lost 104 games and finished last for the first time in their existence. They were 45 games out of first place.

The no-hitters by Trucks were the story of the Tiger season. His first one came on May 15 against Washington at Briggs Stadium in Detroit. Only 2,200 fans were there. Trucks fanned Mickey Vernon for the last out in the top of the ninth. He had no-hit the Senators, but the score was still 0–0. However, in the Tiger ninth, with two out, Vic Wertz hit a Bob Porterfield pitch into the seats. The Tigers had a 1–0 win and Trucks had his no-hitter.

Trucks almost didn't get his second no-hitter that year because of a scoring controversy. Pitching at Yankee Stadium on August 25, Trucks got by the first two innings with ease. In the third inning, Phil Rizzuto of the Yanks hit a grounder to Tiger shortstop Johnny Pesky. Pesky fielded the ball cleanly, but dropped it before throwing to first. Official scorer John Drebinger ruled it an error, then changed his decision ruling the play a hit. But, wait a minute. In the seventh inning, Drebinger called the Tiger dugout and talked with Pesky about the play. Pesky told the writer that he failed to get a grip on the ball and it should be an error. The scorer reversed himself yet again and Trucks still had a no-hit game in his grasp.

It wouldn't be easy. He came to the ninth with the Yankees still without a hit, but he had to face Mickey Mantle, Joe Collins and Hank Bauer.

Trucks reached back for his best fastball and struck out Mantle. Collins lined out to left. Now, he had only Hank Bauer to retire. Bauer hit a hard one-hopper to Al Federoff at second base. Al backed up, grabbed the ball and threw him out at first. Trucks had his second no-hitter in an otherwise mediocre season.

His near third no-hitter? This one happened at Briggs Stadium against Washington. Ed Yost led off the game for the Senators with a line single over third. Trucks then set down the next 27 batters to win a shutout victory. He missed his third no-hitter because of Yost's lead-off single.

Some record, though, for a bad team: two no-hitters and almost a third. If Virgil had accomplished that third no-hitter, he would have been the only pitcher in history to get three in one season.

Trucks had a 17-year pitching career—12 of those years with the Tigers. He pitched for the Tigers in the 1945 World Series against the Cubs and had a victory in that classic. Virgil also pitched for the St. Louis Browns, the White Sox, the Kansas City A's and the Yankees.

But he's best remembered as a Tiger and the man who pitched two no-hitters—and almost a third—in the terrible Tiger year of 1952.

Baseball contracts these days have become so complicated that players get interest-free loans, housing deals, limo service and all kinds of other concessions from the owners.

But there's really nothing new ... even the old-timers had their unique deals. For instance, there was once an American League pitcher whose contract read that he did not have to pitch against the Tigers. His name was Harry "Cy" Morgan, a native of Pomeroy, Ohio.

The crazy contract clause came about this way. Morgan, as a pitcher for the Red Sox, liked to brush back batters. One day in Boston he threw at the Tigers' leadoff man, Davy Jones. Davy walked with his bat in his hand toward the mound to challenge Morgan. He told the pitcher he was going to bunt the next pitch toward first. And if Morgan came over to field the bunt, he would run over him. Jones bunted, but Morgan didn't come near the ball and Jones beat out the bunt for a hit.

The same thing happened between Ty Cobb and Morgan. Again Morgan failed to meet the challenge.

Boston manager Fred Lake had had enough. He cursed Morgan, ran him off the field and later released him. Morgan went to Philadelphia and signed with Connie Mack.

But his contract there was different. He insisted on inserting a clause that Mack would never pitch him in a

game against the Tigers. He wanted no part of Davy
Jones, Ty Cobb or the rest of that gang.

That was 1909. Morgan won 16 games the rest of that
year for the A's. Next season, he won 18. But Mack released him in 1913, after he had won only three in 1912.

Not a bad pitcher, Harry Morgan. But he didn't want
to face the Tigers ... and his contract with the A's said
he didn't have to.

Rube Waddell compiled the greatest major-league
strikeout record over a seven-year period: He fanned
1,808. He also struck out 16 Athletics in one game and for
many years that stood as a record. He still holds the
mark, along with Walter Johnson, for the most strikeouts
in two straight games—he whiffed 26 in 1903.

But the record books don't tell the real story of Rube
Waddell. His story is told by the thousands of old-time
fans and ballplayers who knew the Rube. He was the
most eccentric, the most irresponsible man who ever
spiked a major-league diamond. He was the terror of all
his managers and was unpopular with fellow players.
But strangely enough, Rube was the idol of the fans.

The most famous legend of the Rube is one you'll more
than likely recognize. It happened back in 1901 when he
was a pitcher for Milwaukee. He called the entire team
off the field with the exception of his catcher. And then
the Rube bore down and struck out the first three men
that faced him.

Waddell always insisted that he had lots of speed. One
day in a chat with his next-day opponents, some of the
boys started kidding the Rube. One of the players winked
and said: "Say, Rube, you ain't got so much speed." Well,
Waddell insisted he had plenty of speed, and the players
challenged Rube to go out to the ballpark the next morning and demonstrate his effectiveness. The Rube was
slated to pitch that afternoon but nevertheless he fell for

the gag. He went out in the morning and whipped the
ball from center field to home plate for more than an
hour. It would have ruined any other pitcher, but not
Waddell. He pitched that very same afternoon and won
his ball game.

The Rube was one of the early "bad boys of baseball,"
and only Connie Mack knew how to handle him. Even
the ever-patient Mack finally gave up, but then that's
another story. Rube was a big, strapping left-hander, and
yet his mind was that of a 15-year-old. He constantly
broke training rules and was one of the hardest men to
handle in the history of baseball. However, when the
Rube had all his stuff, he was unhittable.

Waddell got his first trial with Louisville in the old
National League in 1897. He joined Detroit the next year
and jumped the club when he was fined $50. And that
was the beginning of a long, hard career.

He next went to a semi-pro team in Chatham, Ontario.
One of the games he pitched there was a masterpiece:
The Rube fanned 17, threw out nine men at first base and
made the hit that won the game, 1–0. The very next day
he pitched again. And this time he allowed three hits and
struck out 20.

In 1899 the Rube joined Columbus and settled down to
hard work. He won 26 and lost six ... and struck out 200
batters. From Columbus, Waddell was sold to Pittsburgh,
but he put in most of the season with Milwaukee. And it
was here that he first came under the watchful eye of
Connie Mack.

The Rube made a great showing with Milwaukee. One
day in particular stands out in that season of 1900—
August 18. The Rube pitched and won the first game of
a double-header 3–2, in 17 long innings. Then he went
back for the nightcap and hurled a one-hit shutout in a
five-inning game. But the Rube, eccentric as ever,
jumped Milwaukee and in 1901 he pitched first for Pittsburgh and then for Chicago.

At the end of that season, two all-star teams from the American and National leagues toured the country. On the American League team was a player named Harry Davis. And pitching for the Nationals was our old friend Rube Waddell.

After the tour was over, Davis knew that Connie Mack, who'd just been named manager of the A's, was looking for pitching talent. He suggested the Rube. "Not a chance," said Connie. "I can't depend on him." But Davis insisted and Connie found a spot for the "Bad Boy of Baseball." Waddell joined the A's carrying a $1 suitcase filled with $40 worth of fishing tackle.

With his great curve and a blistering fastball, the Rube made his reputation almost overnight. He fanned up to 10, 12, 14 men each game. He won a 17-inning game from Boston, fanning 16. And then, he disappeared. Where he went, nobody knew. Finally, they found the Rube tending a bar in Camden, New Jersey. He was also pitching for a semi-pro team there.

The next year Rube teamed with catcher Ossee Schreckengost in one of the weirdest batteries in baseball—both were clowns and made a great hit with the fans.

The A's won the pennant in 1905 and were to meet the Giants in the World Series. Here was what the fans had been waiting for —a chance to see the great Rube Waddell face the great Christy Mathewson. But the unpredictable Rube broke up the possible duel by a bit of skylarking. As the A's train left Boston, the Rube tripped over Andy Coakley's bag and hurt his pitching arm. He was out of the Series.

Stories came out later that the Rube had been bribed, but they were all proved false. Anyhow, the fans of 1905 missed what could have been the hottest pitching duel in a World Series. The Giants went on to win the classic with Mathewson whitewashing the A's three times.

In 1906, the Rube was all right again. He won 15 games

and lost 17, pitching eight shutouts. But the worry of handling the big boy began to get on Mack's nerves, so he let him go in 1908. He was sold to the Brownies. The first time he pitched against his old teammates, the Rube fanned 16 to beat 'em. By 1909, the Rube had pitched himself out. The ravages of dissipation had ruined what might have been an even more brilliant career. He pitched a few games in 1910 and was then released to Newark. He spent the next three seasons in the minors. But in 1913 his health failed and he virtually collapsed.

The Rube was given money to go to San Antonio to try to regain his health. However, the end came on April 1, 1914. Waddell, only 37 years old, died in a strange town, an unknown pauper. He was buried with only a rough wooden board to mark his grave. Thus, the man who once had the world in his big left hand was laid away. His fine, sturdy physique was only a shadow.

But a year later, his grave was discovered and baseball men in Texas raised funds to build a six-foot shaft in honor of the man who might have been even greater. He was a strange, colorful character ... a character who, despite all his peculiar habits and his infantile antics, was beloved by all the baseball fans who knew him. And his record ... well, that speaks for itself.

Question: Has there ever been a pitcher in the big leagues who pitched both right- and left-handed in regular season games?

Answer: Yes. And the man's name was Anthony J. Mullane. Not only was Tony Mullane a very fine ambidextrous pitcher, he also was the No. 1 matinee idol of his baseball era. Tony was tall and handsome and sported a fancy mustache. Known as "The Count," he also was a talented ice skater, roller skater, boxer and musician. Whenever Tony was announced as the pitcher, a large number of ladies added their presence to the crowd at the park.

In fact, some of the clubs he pitched for allowed the ladies in at special prices when Mullane worked on the mound—a forerunner of our present ladies day.

When he was through pitching, Tony stayed in baseball and managed the Detroit Tigers in 1898.

He was a Tiger relief pitcher in the days when relievers were not really recognized as great contributors. His name was Elon Chester Hogsett, better known as "Chief." He spent 20 years in professional baseball—11 in the American League.

The Chief was born in Brownell, Kansas and grew up on a farm. He found in baseball a way to escape the life of a farmer. After pitching in high school, he turned to semi-pro ball. He pitched for an Independence, Kansas team and was soon released. He then joined a Cushing, Oklahoma pro team.

A Tiger scout taught the Chief to throw a change-up. He signed with the Tigers and after four minor-league seasons was promoted to the parent team. Hogsett made his Tiger debut in 1929 as a starter against Washington. The Senators beat him, 2–0, in a double-header in which the Tigers failed to score in both games.

In 1930 Hogsett moved to the bullpen. He was unusual: He was a left-handed sinker-ball pitcher who threw with a side-arm motion. It was as a reliever that the Chief helped the Tigers win pennants in 1934 and '35. He worked relief for Detroit in both of those World Series.

In 1936 Hogsett was traded away from the Tigers because of an injury—although not his own. Detroit first baseman Hank Greenberg was hurt early in the '36 season and Hogsett was traded to the Browns for first baseman Jack Burns. Hogsett was with Washington by 1938 and then went back to the minors. He appeared again with the Tigers in 1944, when World War II had depleted the big-league rosters.

The Chief was really a man ahead of his time. Now, the bullpen pitchers are superstars. They make the headlines and the big money. When Hogsett pitched, a reliever was almost a second-class citizen of baseball.

Not too many years ago the Tigers had a pitcher named Louis Norman "Bobo" Newsom. That's not much news, because Bobo also belonged to seven other big-league clubs in his 25-year baseball career. But Bobo did have two great years with Detroit. He won 20 games in 1939 and in 1940 pitched the Tigers to a pennant with a 21–5 record. He also won two games in the 1940 World Series for Detroit.

Old Bobo was a courageous pitcher and nothing could stop him. On one of the many opening days that he pitched for the Senators in Washington, he was hit in the face with a thrown ball. Although the accident happened in the first inning, Ol' Bobo pitched the rest of the game and won it. After the game was over, it was revealed that Newsom had suffered a broken jaw. He was asked why he hadn't left the game.

"Whenever the President of the United States comes out to watch Ol' Bobo pitch," he said, "Ol' Bobo ain't gonna disappoint him."

In 1940, Newsom beat the Reds in the first game of the World Series. Then his father died. Bobo returned to beat the Reds again in the fourth game. He tried again in the seventh game, but lost 2–1 to Paul Derringer.

"Ol' Bobo sure would have liked to win that one," he said later.

A reporter sensed a story. "Win it for your father?" he prodded.

"No, for Ol' Bobo," the great one replied.

Matt Kilroy, pitching for Baltimore in 1886, struck out 513 hitters. That year the pitching slab was only 50 feet from home plate, and it took seven balls to give a batter a base on balls.

Bill Kennedy of Carnesville, Georgia holds modern baseball's strikeout record of 456 in 1946 for Rocky Mount. He averaged 14.7 strikeouts per nine innings. He later pitched for the Browns, Cleveland, White Sox, Boston and Cincinnati.

In days when pitchers threw at batters, Charlie Grimm batted against Burleigh Grimes. When he went to the plate, Grimm laid down in the batter's box. The umpire, Bill Klem, said, "What are you doing down there?" Grimm said, "Grimes is going to throw at me anyway, so I thought I'd duck early."

Walter "Smoke" Justis, a pitcher for the Tigers in 1905, pitched four no-hitters in the span of two months in 1908 for Lancaster, Ohio.

Sad Sam Jones didn't throw to first base for five years. When he finally did, he had the runner out but the first baseman dropped the ball.

Dizzy Dean once hit seven straight Giants in an exhibition game, and once the regular season got under way, those New Yorkers didn't beat him all that year.

When a reporter asked, "What's your greatest asset?" pitcher Lefty Gomez answered, "Fast outfielders."

Satchel Paige used to say "Throw strikes; home plate don't move."

Pitcher Jim Bunning had an explanation about why to keep the ball down to a hitter: "Have you ever seen a 450-foot ground ball?"

In 1944, Charlie "Red" Barrett of the Boston Braves threw only 58 pitches in a nine-inning game, beating Cincinnati 2–0.

In the early 1900s, the home pitcher pitched batting practice for both teams. Walter Johnson did it in 1907, the day before his debut, which he lost to the Tigers 3–2.

What pitcher with 15 lifetime wins or more has the best record against the Yankees? Tiger Frank Lary at 28–13. Babe Ruth comes in a close second at 15–7.

Warren Spahn and Robin Roberts, two Hall-of-Fame pitchers, were great rivals, but also friends. Warren Spahn's son idolized Roberts. He once told his dad when he was mad at him, "Robin Roberts pitches better than you." And once when he was mad at his mother, he told her, "And Mrs. Roberts cooks better than you do."

In 1908, Washington's Walter Johnson pitched three shutouts in four days, giving up a total of twelve hits. On Friday, he pitched a six-hit shutout; on Saturday, a four-hit shutout; and on Monday (Sunday was an off-day) he came back and pitched a two-hit shutout—all against New York.

EIGHT

A Walk on the Wild Side

"Baseball players are the weirdest of all. I think it's all that organ music."

Peter Gent

For a pitcher to throw at a batter is fairly common practice in professional baseball. But have you ever heard of a bean ball being aimed at a runner on first base?

The man who did it was Charles A. "Buzz" Wetzel while pitching in the Pacific Coast League a good many years ago.

Buzz was trying to bean a certain batter. He threw at him at the plate four times, missing each time. So the batter walked.

As soon as the batter had reached first and taken a short lead, Wetzel fired a throw to first, right at the runner's head. The throw clipped him above the ear and he went down in the dirt, just a few feet off the bag.

Wetzel was still mad, and he yelled at the runner:

"Guess that'll teach you, you lousy so-and-so. Next time you'll stand up at the plate and let me hit you like a man."

Del Wilber was a Detroit Tiger scout, but before he became one he filled many other baseball jobs. Del has been a player, coach and manager. But most of all he is a storyteller and a good one.

"I'm with the Red Sox and we're playing Cleveland," Del begins. "It's the second game of a double-header. Jim Piersall, my Boston teammate, had struck out four times in the first game. Now we're in the second game. Mike Garcia is mowing us down. Already, he has struck out Piersall in his first two times at bat.

"Piersall's due at bat again. I'm on deck and he's at the plate. He has a bat with him at the plate, but he throws it back to me in the on-deck circle. So, I figure he wants my bat. I toss it to him, but he throws it back to me. Now, he gets in the batter's box. But he has no bat. This makes the pitcher Garcia mad. He throws at Jim. Jim ducks. Garcia throws at him again. Mike's so mad he walks Piersall.

"Now I'm at bat. Piersall steals second. He gets to third on a wild pitch. Then I tap a little roller down toward third and get a hit. Piersall scores and that's the winning run.

"I'll never get over Jim, coming to bat without a bat."

Let's tune in Del Wilber again:

"This is in Boston, too. My roommate (I won't name him) had been out all night. It had been a rough time for him. And we had a double-header coming up. He gets into the first game, relieving, and wins the game. Between games, he gets an ice cream cone, eats it and then goes to sleep in the back seat of the bullpen car.

"Now, our starter is getting banged around. And our manager, Lou Boudreau, decides to make a change. He calls for Sid Hudson to come in and relieve. Sid gets in the car and the car heads for the diamond. But nobody knows that my roommate is asleep in the back.

"Well, the car reaches the front of the Red Sox dugout and Hudson steps out to go to the mound. Right behind him my roommate steps out, too. Now we've got two pitchers coming into the game at once.

"Boudreau is going bananas. He sends my roommate back to the car and to the bullpen. My roommate resumes his sleeping in the bullpen. He sleeps for a while and then gets a call to come into the game. This time he actually does come in to pitch and mops up for the Red Sox.

"That was the only time I ever saw two pitchers try to enter a game at the same time."

Injuries happen all the time in baseball and certainly they play a major role in any pennant race. But here's an injury story with a double-twist. Maybe it has happened more than this one time, but I doubt it.

In 1970 the Phillies had two veteran catchers on their roster: Tim McCarver and Mike Ryan. Well, McCarver was catching the Phils this particular night in San Francisco. The Giant hitter was Willie Mays. Willie bailed out on a pitch. As he pulled away, Mays hit the ball on the end of his bat. It came off the bat and hit McCarver flush on the back of his right hand.

McCarver was taken to a San Francisco hospital, and into the game to catch came Mike Ryan.

Just a few minutes later Ryan tagged Willie McCovey at the plate ... and broke his right hand.

When McCarver arrived at the hospital, he knew nothing about the injury to Ryan. He was greeted by a doctor who said, "How are you, Mr. Ryan? We've been expecting you."

McCarver was confused.

"I'm not Ryan," he said. "I'm Tim McCarver. You've got the wrong name."

"But we were told to expect Mr. Ryan," the doctor said. Then he began to treat McCarver, pulling his middle finger back into place.

At that very moment, in walked Mike Ryan with his broken right hand. McCarver says he almost fell over.

Ryan looked at McCarver and said, "You know, Tim, I've been waiting all season for something to happen to you—but now it has to happen to me, too."

It was an oddity, all right: two Phillie catchers breaking their right hands in the same inning and ending up together in the same hospital at the same time.

Will women ever get a chance to play in professional baseball? I don't think so. No woman has ever played in the big leagues . . . and only two have played in a regular minor-league game. Even then, each appearance was a brief one.

Not in almost 40 years has there been an attempt for women to play in organized baseball. In June of 1952, the Harrisburg (Pennsylvania) Senators in the Interstate League announced plans to sign Eleanor Engle to a contract. Eleanor, 24 years old and 132 pounds, was a stenographer at the state capitol. She worked out with the team, but before she could play, National Association President George Trautman quickly issued a rule which barred the signing of women as players.

Since then, nobody has tested that ruling.

There have been several highly publicized cases of female players; but they've been little more than publicity. Mildred "Babe" Didrickson Zaharias, the great all-round athlete, pitched against the Cleveland Indians in an exhibition in the 1930s. And you might remember that in the first night game in Cincinnati in 1935 Paul Derringer of the Reds pitched to a woman who had run to the plate and grabbed a bat.

When I was a youngster in Atlanta, there was a lot of national attention focused on a 17-year-old girl named Jackie Mitchell in Chattanooga. This was the doing of Joe Engel, owner of the Chattanooga Lookouts. Mitchell pitched against the New York Yankees in an exhibition game April 2, 1931. She relieved Clyde Barfoot in the first inning with Babe Ruth coming to bat. She struck out Babe Ruth and Lou Gehrig. Jackie walked Tony Lazzeri and then was taken out of the game by manager Bert Niehoff. Barfoot returned to the mound to retire the side. Joe Engel put Jackie on the Lookouts roster, but she never pitched. Instead, he gave her a job in the promotion department.

The first woman actually to participate in a pro game was Elizabeth Stroud, who played under the name of Lizzie Arlington. Lizzie had pitched and played infield around the sandlot and semi-pro leagues. Lizzie played in one game in the Atlantic League in 1898, playing second and pitching for Reading against the Allentown team. She was supposed to pitch the next day for Hartford, but her appearance was cancelled.

As a buildup—before the cancellation—here's what the Hartford paper wrote: "It is said that she plays ball just like a man and talks ball like a man, and if it was not for her bloomers, she would be taken for a man on the diamond, having none of the peculiarities of women ballplayers."

Other games had been planned for Lizzie, but they never happened and she faded into oblivion after that one appearance.

The only other time a woman appeared in the lineup of a minor-league team was on September 7, 1936, in Fayetteville, Arkansas, in the Class D Arkansas-Mis-

souri League. Frances Dunlop played right field for Fayetteville, failed to get a hit in three times at bat and
made a fine running catch. She is the only female to play
an entire game in the professional ranks.

If you look in the *Encyclopedia of Baseball,* you'll see the
name of Ed Linke. It won't tell you much in the pitcher
register of that book, only that he pitched for two big-
league teams—Washington and the St. Louis Browns—
and won 22 and lost 22.

It certainly doesn't tell you that Ed Linke figured in
one of the freakiest double plays ever. It happened during
Ed's most successful season with Washington, 1935, the
year he won 11 and lost 7.

The Senators were playing the Yankees at Yankee
Stadium. The Yanks' Ben Chapman, a speedy runner,
was on second. The batter was Jesse Hill. Linke threw
Hill a fastball. Hill swung and hit a solid line drive toward the pitcher's box. The drive hit Linke squarely on
the forehead as he was finishing his follow-through.
Linke fell and was out cold. The ball ricocheted off his
forehead back toward home plate.

Jack Redmond, the Washington catcher, caught the
ball on the fly and fired to second to double-off Chapman.
By using his head, Linke had started an unusual double
play.

Was he hurt? Not badly. He was out for about 45 seconds and ended up with a big knot on his forehead. He
spent three weeks in a New York hospital, then returned
for pitching duty with the Senators and was no worse for
wear.

Linke lasted six years in the American League—five
with Washington and a final season with the St. Louis
Browns. Like many, his career was cut short by a sore
arm.

Everybody in baseball knows you have to expect the unexpected at all times. You never know what might happen.

This one happened on a strikeout in a Cubs-Dodger game during the 1916 season. Casey Stengel was the authority, and as Casey used to say, "You can look it up."

The Cubs were at Ebbets Field in Brooklyn. Their batter, Rollie Zeider struck out. The pitch got by the Brooklyn catcher and hit the umpire, Mal Eason, in the chest. The ball rebounded toward third base.

There Mike Mowrey, the Brooklyn third baseman, picked up the ball off the grass and fired it to first in time to retire the batter Zeider, running to first after he had fanned.

A crazy, unexpected way to get a man out. And the Brooklyn third baseman, Mowrey, was credited with an assist on the strikeout.

Baseball has seen some big eaters. Many a would-be star has literally eaten himself out of the big leagues. Shanty Hogan, of the New York Giants, couldn't stay away from the table, and many others like him have failed to make the grade because they could never control their caloric intake.

In the early 1970s, the New York Yankees had a young first baseman, Ron Blomberg, and they bet on Ron every time in the knife-and-fork league. One year in spring training, one of those "ALL YOU CAN EAT FOR $4.95" restaurants was forced to bar Blomberg from its premises because his gigantic appetite threatened to put the restaurant out of business.

Ron may hold the modern baseball record for eating. He admits that once in a contest in Atlanta, his hometown, he consumed at one sitting a total of 28 hamburgers.

Collecting bubble-gum cards of major-league players is one of the world's most popular hobbies. But not many collectors in 1969 realized that one of their cards showed a picture of a bat boy instead of a player.

When the photographer for Topps Bubble Gum Company visited the camp of the California Angels that spring, he mistook the Angel bat boy for infielder Aurelio Rodriguez. He snapped the picture of the bat boy and submitted it to his company.

And in every set of cards that season, there was no photo of Rodriguez on his card. Instead, there was the picture of the Angel bat boy, misidentified as Aurelio Rodriguez.

While this story is only 20 years old, it has the feel of something which might have happened back in the early days of baseball, when the atmosphere was more informal and relaxed and when events sometimes took a turn on the spur of the moment.

Scipio Spinks, the young pitcher for the St. Louis Cardinals, was sitting in the stands on a May day in the early 1970s in civilian clothes, charting the pitches during the Card game with Atlanta. Then in the sixth inning, manager Red Schoendienst of the Cards decided he needed a pinch runner. He knew that Spinks was a one-time track star at Harlan High in Chicago, so he summoned the youngster from the stands for running duty.

Spinks put up his clipboard, headed to the clubhouse and dressed in his Cardinal baseball uniform. He then entered the game in the ninth inning as a pinch runner for Joe Hague and scored the tying run. St. Louis scored three times in that inning and beat the Braves, 5–4.

Tucked away in the rolling, red hills of Georgia is the town of Royston. It gave to baseball one of the game's great stars. It gave to medicine an eminent physician-surgeon.

The fiery genius of the baseball star blazed across the nation's headlines. But the doctor turned down numerous remunerative offers and remained in Royston, serving his own people and the many who came from other parts of the South to benefit from his skill.

These two who were boyhood friends got together again to plan a hospital which the baseball star gave to Royston as a memorial to his parents. As they planned, their thoughts relived the days when they swam, fished and played baseball together. Their chief interests, even then, were baseball and medicine. The ambition of one was to become a star in the major leagues; the other wanted to be an outstanding doctor.

However, fate plays tricks.

The boy who hoped to be the baseball star was Dr. Stewart D. Brown, the fine physician-surgeon; and the youngster who dreamed of a medical career was Ty Cobb, the greatest baseball star of all time.

Guy Hecker, the old-time Louisville star, once played several games without a shirt. Twenty-five ladies wrote letters of protest, and he put the shirt on again.

George Sisler, first baseman for the St. Louis Browns, threw to first in a game against the Yankees and the pitcher didn't cover. Sisler raced after his own toss, picked up the ball and touched the base ahead of the runner.

Joe McCarthy played at Louisville with rough thumb nails. If the pitch came close, he'd yell that he'd been hit. Actually he would run his thumb nail across his hand as he hit the ground and would come up bleeding. He got a free trip to first base many times that way.

Ray Murray was an old character who caught for the Orioles and, at one time, in the minor leagues for Oklahoma City. Somebody hit a foul pop fly. Ray lost it and it dropped at his feet. Murray stood there, looked at the ball for a minute, then crouched down and walked around it like he was stalking it. All of a sudden he pounced on it like a big cat, stuck the ball under his leg, dug a hole with his hands, shoved the ball in the hole and covered it with dirt. Then he patted the dirt down, asked the umpire for another ball and went back to catching.

In Brooklyn, Charlie Dressen brought in Clyde King to stop a rally. Clyde met Charlie and Pee Wee Reese at the mound and told them he wasn't ready. When King completed his allotted warm-up tosses, Reese went back to shortstop and acted as if he had something in his eye so Clyde could throw more warm-up pitches. The plan didn't work, though, because King walked over to Pee Wee to see if he could help him with his eye.

Germany Schaefer of the Tigers played the sixth inning of the July 3, 1906 game in Cleveland in a raincoat. The game was eventually called because of rain.

Joe Warrick, third baseman for Louisville in 1886, played a full game wearing an overcoat. He had a chill and had to put on the overcoat. He had a few fielding chances and played very well. But at the plate, he was 0 for 3, so in the ninth, he took off the coat and hit a triple.

An American League game was once called because of wind. When Texas played Toronto on April 30, 1984, winds gusted to 35 mph. Doug Rader of Texas pulled Frank Tanana as starter and went with Jim Bibby—the heaviest pitcher in the league at 250. No way he'd be blown around. Play eventually was called by umpire Don Denkinger.

Has a player ever caught his own home run? In 1946 at Ebbets Field, Dixie Walker's home run stuck in the right field screen. At the end of that inning, Dixie went to his position in right field, and when the ball dropped out of the screen, Dixie caught it.

When Chicago Cub batter Moe Drabowski was hit on the foot by a pitch, teammate Dick Drott borrowed a wheelchair from a crippled fan and rolled it to the plate. He told Drabowski to get in it and wheeled him to first base. The umpire was Stan Landes. He was not amused and gave Drott the thumb.

Rube Waddell owned a mockingbird until it irritated his teammates so much that one of them strangled it.

NINE

Did You Hear the One About ...

"They say you can't do it, but sometimes it doesn't always work."

Casey Stengel

Don Larsen will be best remembered as the New York Yankee pitcher who hurled the only perfect game in World Series history. But those who knew him well will cherish the impression of Don as a big, happy-go-lucky guy who loved to have his fun and was always able to take anything in stride.

Larsen had experienced some lean years and some good ones. Yet all of a sudden, fame was thrust upon him because of his perfect game. He made some early appearances on TV and radio, and, of course, all kinds of promoters began to suggest all kinds of plans to make Mr. Larsen a very rich man.

One of these promoters came to Larsen with grandiose ideas. After a quick introduction to the big guy, he said to Don, "Don, now just suppose one morning you woke up and found $90,000 in your pants pocket. What would you think?"

"What would I think?" answered Don. "I'd think that I had on somebody else's pants."

The colorful ex-major-league pitcher Bobo Newsom never lacked an alibi. Once while pitching for the Browns, Newsom was losing, 15–0. Somebody asked him, "What's wrong, Bobo?"

"What's wrong?" he shot back. I'll tell you what's wrong. How's any pitcher ever gonna win a game for a team when they can't get you no runs?"

Later in his career, when Bobo was pitching for Washington, a reporter asked him about his 1948 record. Newsom told the reporter he had pitched the opening game that season for the Giants and had beaten the Boston Braves, 1–0. Later, the reporter checked the official record books and found that Bobo had not won a game during the entire 1948 season. He told Newsom about his findings.

Ol' Bobo still had an answer. He said: "That's not the way I remember it, but let it be. It's too late now to change a mistake in print like that."

Yogi Berra has been in the Baseball Hall of Fame at Cooperstown, New York, for almost 20 years now and, though the selection lends a certain amount of dignity to Yogi's image, he is still the same old Yogi. No matter what heights he reaches, he'll always do something different and picturesque, and the Yogi Berra stories will always be a part of the lore of baseball.

Some years back, in St. Louis, Yogi was interviewed on a radio show by Jack Buck who was a longtime friend.

All guests on the show received a $25 check made out "Payable to the Bearer," spelled B-E-A-R-E-R. When

Yogi received his check after the show, he complained to his announcer friend. "How can you do this? You've known me all these years and you spell my name like that?"

Signals sometimes can be a baffling part of baseball— even to the players. Cesar Tovar of the Minnesota Twins was having trouble remembering his team's signals, so manager Bill Rigney came up with a simple solution. "Cesar," he said, "the steal sign will be on whenever you hear the coach call you by your last name."

"Okay, I understand," Tovar told his manager.

Tovar got on first soon after this instruction. Coach Vern Morgan put on the steal sign by yelling: "All right, Tovar, stay alive. Come on Tovar. The old hustle, Tovar. Let's go, Tovar."

Suddenly Cesar called time. He went over to the coach and said, "What's this Tovar business? I've been with this club seven years and you're still calling me by my last name."

If you ever saw a sawed-off piece of dynamite glide under a pop fly, wait, then take it in with a vest-pocket catch, Walter "Rabbit" Maranville's name should bring back a thousand memories.

Rabbit was an old-school player. But although he started in the rough-tough days, he played long enough for his service to overlap into the more modern game. Maranville's greatest diamond fame came during the 1914 season when he was sparking those fabulous Boston Braves to the National League pennant.

There are countless stories about the Rabbit—a clown and a guy who lived for fun and very little else.

Once the Rabbit dove into the goldfish pond in the lobby of a Cincinnati hotel. Three old maids in the lobby were astonished to see the Rabbit in a snappy business suit, stepping out of the pond with a celluloid goldfish in his mouth.

The most memorable story about the Rabbit, though, concerned the hidden-ball trick—that ancient annoyance to any baseball player, but especially to an alert star like Maranville.

The Braves were playing in Cincinnati in the early '30s. It was the eighth inning, two out and the score tied. Maranville was the third hitter, and he cracked a double into left field. The ball was thrown in to Joe Stripp at third, and somehow he managed to slip it along to second baseman Tony Cuccinello.

Maranville was paying no attention to this maneuver. He was too busy telling umpire Bill Klem what a great hitter a guy named Maranville was.

The pitcher walked over near the slab and pretended to be ready to face the next batter. Maranville wandered off second, taking a nice lead: After all, he was to be the tie-breaking run.

About this time, second baseman Cuccinello walked over and said: "Look what I've got, Rabbit."

Tony touched Maranville and the inning and the scoring threat were over . . . snuffed out by the old hidden-ball trick.

Maranville was sorer than a hammered finger. The fact that the battle went 12 innings that torrid afternoon, coupled with the fact that the Braves lost to Cincinnati, didn't make him any happier. He returned to his hotel in a foul mood.

Now Mr. Maranville was fond of cantaloupe. In fact, he liked the stuff so much that everybody in the league knew it, including the Cincinnati players. So, armed with this information, the rival Cincinnati boys decided to play another hidden-ball trick—with a slightly different flavor. They arranged to have Maranville's regular waiter in the hotel dining room conceal a baseball in a cantaloupe which had been cut in two and carefully reamed out. The baseball was inscribed "Cucinello to Maranville."

When Rabbit picked up the top of the cantaloupe—the part he thought was filled with ice—the baseball greeted him. This repeat performance of the afternoon's trick was even less funny to the Rabbit. His temper flared. Without thinking, he grabbed the ball and threw it hard and straight, right at the retreating waiter, who was leaving the busy dining room for the kitchen. Maranville's control was perfect and the ball hit the waiter on the back of the ear. The waiter grabbed the back of his head and slumped to the floor—out cold for an hour.

Fortunately for the thus-far unfortunate Maranville, the man was a baseball bug. He held no animosity toward the Rabbit; in fact, he came to Maranville and asked for the ball which had victimized him.

"Rabbit," he told the ballplayer. "I want that ball. I am the only guy who's ever been able to pull the hidden-ball trick on you for the second time in the same day."

Maranville gave the waiter the famous ball and later capped it off by giving him a season pass.

Minnie Minoso, the White Sox coach, was an outstanding American League outfielder. In his heyday in the '50s and '60s, he spoke Spanish most of the time, but he also spoke English.

Once a female reporter was interviewing Minnie before a game. This time he spoke English. Near the end of the interview, the reporter asked Minoso who he thought was the American League's best outfielder.

His answer? "Minoso."

She was somewhat surprised that he would nominate himself, and she pressed the issue.

"Are you sure?" she asked.

Minnie came back with a quick reply: "Me know so."

Alibis are a dime a dozen in baseball, but sometimes a player will reach fantastic heights in quest of an excuse.

Early in the 1970s, Chicago Cub Joe Pepitone was having a batting slump—one of those periods when nothing went right. He came to bat in a tight spot for the Cubs. Two men on and two out. The count went to 3 and 2. The Pirate pitcher, Nelson Briles, fired a hard, high pitch over the head of Pepitone. Overanxious, he swung at the wild delivery and missed.

As he walked back to the Cub dugout, Pepitone muttered to teammate Ron Santo, "How can any major-league pitcher be that wild on a 3-and-2 pitch?"

It's been a long-standing gag in baseball and in radio and TV: "Didn't you used to be Paul Carey?" Or (while you're talking to Merle Harmon) you say, "Whatever happened to Merle Harmon?"

I actually had it happen to me.

During World War II, I broadcast the Atlanta Cracker baseball games in the Southern League before the Marine Corps decided I'd do better at Camp LeJeune, North Carolina. The manager at that time was a chubby first baseman named Harry Hughes. Harry had banged around the minors for many seasons and was a stop-gap manager for the Crackers.

Well, after a month of broadcasting, I was in North Carolina with the Marines. From there I was sent to Washington and then shipped overseas as sports editor and correspondent for *Leatherneck,* the Marine magazine.

The Navy ship dropped me off at Honolulu and my first station was Camp Catlin. Incidentally, the camp team had a young shortstop named Alvin Dark who was about the hottest thing around since the Springfield '03 rifle. The first game I saw Alvin play, he made three errors at short and the hotshot didn't look so hot to me. Anyway, I did an article on him—most of it about his football days at LSU.

There were other fine ballplayers at Camp Catlin— some from the big leagues and many others from the minors.

One of the first places I checked into was the mess hall where these Marine ballplayers ate. There I ran across my old buddy, Harry Hughes, the man who had managed the Crackers when I was announcing their games.

"Hi, Harry," I greeted him.

"How ya doing?" he answered. "Have a seat."

Chow was over. Most of the other guys had gone back to their barracks. Harry and I sat there and chatted. We talked about those Cracker days. Incidentally, Roy Hartsfield, the one-time Blue Jay manager, was a 17-year-old rookie shortstop on that team.

I asked about old so-and-so. And Harry would fill me in on the details of where he was now and what he was doing. He asked me about some of the sportswriters and the radio people he had known around the Atlanta sports scene.

We got ourselves another cup of coffee and started on another round of conversation. We were whipping along in great fashion—two old pals who hadn't seen each other in a couple of years, both of us away from home and both of us very lonely.

We'd been talking about 40 minutes and Harry Hughes looked me right in the eye and said: "By the way, whatever happened to Ernie Harwell?"

I almost fell off the bench.

After recovering, I told him I was Ernie Harwell.

"I don't believe it," he said.

I showed him my ID card.

"I still don't believe it, but I guess you are Ernie Harwell after all," he told me.

I think of that whenever I run across that old gag, "Whatever happened to ... ?"

Rollie Hemsley, the old-time catcher, was a real prank-
ster in his day. When Rollie was with the St. Louis
Browns, his manager was the great Rogers Hornsby.
Once in a while, Hemsley would get out of hand, and his
manager would have to crack down on him.

One evening on the train, Rollie was having his fun
by putting live frogs in the pullman berth of each
player—and the manager. Hornsby grabbed him and told
him he was fined $50. Hemsley went to the observation
car, borrowing some knitting from an old lady on the
way. He proceeded to knit in the corner of the car until
manager Hornsby came along. When Hornsby saw that
scene he exploded and fined Hemsley another $50—this
time for knitting.

Sparky Lyle—the great New York Yankee relief
pitcher—saved 35 games in 1972—then a major-league
record. Hardly a game went by without Sparky marching
in to take over his relief assignment. Each starting Yankee pitcher knew that should he falter even slightly, Lyle
would finish the game.

One night several of the Yank pitchers were enjoying
their steaks in a downtown restaurant. One turned to the
others and said, "It's a good thing Sparky Lyle's not here
with us tonight. He'd finish eating all these steaks for
us."

The days of the Dodgers in Brooklyn are legendary ...
especially when Wilbert Robinson was managing the
team. The Dodgers back then never went anywhere, but
they were a fun-loving outfit who played the game about
as loose as any team ever listed in the standings.

One afternoon at old Ebbets Field, the Dodgers began
to rally. A couple of hits, a walk, another hit and the

runs were coming home. It was a chance to get back in the game.

A young, enthusiastic Brooklyn bench-warmer grabbed a bat and began to beat it on the dugout steps. He wanted to rattle the Cardinal pitcher and make some noise for his own side.

Suddenly his manager, Wilbert Robinson, turned to the rookie and said: "Cut it out."

"Why?" asked the bewildered cheerleader.

"Lissen, son," answered Robby, "Ol' Jesse Petty is sleeping over there in the corner, and we sure don't want to wake up Ol' Jesse, do we?"

It's no secret that baseball managers have a tendency to exaggerate. When he managed the Reds in 1958, Birdie Tebbetts gave in to such a temptation.

Birdie telephoned Paul Richards, the Baltimore manager, and finally traced him to a Detroit golf course. As Richards finished the 14th hole, the pro rode up and said: "You're wanted on long distance. It's Birdie Tebbetts. He says this is the most important call of your life."

The statement compelled Richards to ride back to the clubhouse to speak with Tebbetts.

When he returned, he was disgusted. Tebbetts merely wanted Richards to let waivers through on Walt Dropo of the White Sox, so the Reds could grab him.

"Well," grunted Richards to his foursome, "if that's the most important call in my life, I'm in trouble."

Chico Carrasquel put in some great seasons with the Chicago White Sox during the 1950s. And naturally there was a great pride in Chico in his native Venezuela. Whenever Chico did anything, it was a headline in Venezuela.

Writers in Venezuela didn't get to Chicago often, so

they covered the exploits of their countryman by phone. One year Chico was playing short for manager Marty Marion and not hitting at all. The writers in Venezuela suspected dissension between Chico and his manager or perhaps with someone else. So, to clear up the matter, they telephoned the White Sox general manager, Frank Lane.

A writer asked Lane, "Are Marty Marion and Carrasquel having trouble?"

Frank's answer was "No."

Next question: "Are you and Chico having trouble?"

Again the answer was "No."

Another question: "Is Chico having trouble with anybody?"

This time Lane came back, "Yes, he's having lots of trouble with the American League pitchers."

In an intra-squad game with the Dodgers, Norm Sherry was sent sprawling in the dirt by a pitch from his brother, Larry Sherry. "I couldn't believe it. I got up and dusted myself off and yelled at him, 'Do that again, and I'll call Mom.'"

A Baltimore writer asked manager Cap Anson to wire an estimate of the Orioles' pennant chances in 50 words. The reply came in one word—none.

When Ralph Houk was managing at Denver in the mid-'50s, he once told an umpire, "I'm not allowed to cuss, but I'd thought you'd like to know that on the way to the game today I passed a kennel and your mother is all right."

Tigers Charlie Gehringer and Chief Hogsett were perfect roommates—neither ever talked. They only had one falling out. At breakfast one day, Hogsett leaned across the table and said, "Charlie, please pass the salt." Gehringer stiffened, but made no effort to oblige. Finally Hogsett asked, "Did I say anything wrong, Charlie?" "You could have pointed," Charlie replied.

Yogi Berra used to love money. Somebody asked what he would do if he found a million bucks. "If the guy who lost it was real poor, I'd give it back to him," Yogi said.

Manager Frankie Frisch lost his cap running and wondered why it happened all the time. John E. "Beans" Reardon, the old umpire and a great opponent of Frankie's, said, "It's simple enough, Frank. You can't put a round cap on a square head."

One year, in the early '80s, Mike Armstrong and Bill Castro were warming up in the Kansas City bullpen and the phone rang. It was Cloyd Boyer, the pitching coach. He asked Jim Schaffer who was ready. "They're both ready," came the reply. Then Boyer said, "Which one looks better?" And Schaffer said, "They're both ugly."

Casey Stengel had this advice for a soldier who had criticized his managerial strategy: "If you're so smart, Buster, let's see you get out of the Army."

Jerome Holtzman, the Chicago writer, once asked White Sox pitcher Ray Moore one of the stock phrases of spring training: "Did you have a good winter?" Ray said, "I always have a good winter, it's my summers that are lousy."

Somebody asked Miller Huggins, the Yankee manager, "What does a player need the most in a slump?" Huggins answered, "A string of good alibis."

TEN

Black Cats and Broken Mirrors

"I have only one superstition. I make sure to touch all the bases when I hit a home run."

Babe Ruth

When the Boston Braves miracle team of 1914 made baseball history with its furious dash from last place in the National League to a world's championship, its pilot was George Stallings, one of the most superstitious men in diamond annals.

On the afternoon the Bostons started their famous comeback, Stallings, because of the big crowd at the game and the heavy traffic, was forced to park his automobile two long blocks from the field. From that day until the end of the season, even if a post was available almost in front of the park, he backed his car into the same place. He would never tempt the whammy by changing his habits while the Braves were winning.

Once during a game, Stallings bent over to tie a shoelace. Just at that moment the Braves burst into a 10-run rally. The manager maintained his cramped position until the last man was out. Yes, the Bostons won. But Stallings had to be carried to the clubhouse where a trainer untangled his hex-bound muscles.

George's number one allergy was a scrap of paper. Never would he allow even a very small bit in front of the Brave bench. His bat boy had a standing order to keep that territory entirely free of such trash.

During the 1914 dash, Stallings ran into special trouble in Philadelphia. Sherwood Magee of the Phils knew of the manager's phobia and tipped off the local fans. They sat behind the Boston dugout and deliberately tore up paper, just to get George's goat. But he put a stop to that. During the last two series in Philadelphia, Stallings bought out all the seats near his dugout.

Indeed, here was a man who would not only undergo physical discomfort, but even pay out money to chase a jinx.

Major leaguers still have their superstitions, but they're nothing like they were in the days before so many collegians infiltrated the ranks.

Chief Myers, the old catcher, used to think there were exactly 100 hits in each bat. Second baseman Hughie Critz would always fill his pockets with dirt for good luck.

The Pirates' great outfielder, Max Carey, would always kick third base as he trotted to his outfield position. Once his Pittsburgh teammates decided to play a trick on Max. As they started onto the field, they all gathered at third base and made a circle so Max couldn't get through to touch the bag.

The umpire Bill Klem got a little impatient. The players wouldn't let Carey through their cordon and Carey wouldn't go to his position until he had completed his ritual.

Finally, Klem issued an order to the players: "All

right, that's enough," he said. "Let him touch the base so we can play ball."

In their pennant-winning years of 1934 and '35, the Tigers had a veteran pitcher who was not as publicized as Schoolboy Rowe or Tommy Bridges, but who was a steady, dependable performer. His name was Alvin Crowder, better known as "General" Crowder. The General had pitched for Washington and for the Browns and had three times won more than 20 games. His best year with the Tigers was 1935, when he turned in 16 victories.

But our story about Crowder concerns his great superstition, and it happened when he pitched for Washington. When Crowder broke into the majors at Washington, the great Walter Johnson was finishing his brilliant career there. One season Crowder was having tough luck. He lost his first four games. Disgusted, he gave away his glove, figuring it was bad luck for him. Johnson, meanwhile, was still winning. So Crowder went to Johnson and asked the veteran to let him use his glove. Johnson obliged. Crowder used Johnson's glove and won. He pitched again with Johnson's glove and won again. He never said anything about returning the glove to Johnson. Walter's good luck charm was his strong right arm. Besides, he was a number one gentleman, so he pitched his own games with another glove.

Crowder kept pitching and winning—with Johnson's glove. Then in Cleveland one day, Crowder was called from the bullpen to relieve Earl Whitehill. He had not taken the lucky glove to the bullpen, so he sent the batboy to the clubhouse to get it from a trunk where he had hidden it. For five minutes the boy looked and couldn't find the glove. The game was held up since Crowder refused to pitch without the glove. He went into the clubhouse himself and searched. Finally he came out on the field with the glove—and a look of relief.

He kept pitching with it and winning. He had built up a streak of 15 games when the season ended. Then, he nursed Johnson's glove all winter. Come the new season, Crowder went to the mound with the lucky glove—but this time he lost. After the game, he rushed up to Johnson and yelled at him with anger: "Here, Walter, take your glove—it's bad luck."

It seems to me that every team is always looking for a left-hand starting pitcher. And rightly so: They are hard to find.

But there was a ballplayer a good many years ago who didn't care if he ever saw a left-hand pitcher. His name was John King, a colorful minor-leaguer who played in the Texas, East Texas and Southern leagues. John never made the big leagues but became a legend simply because of his intense hatred of left-handers.

When King's first son was born, he had to make sure the baby would not grow up to be left-handed. He was shocked speechless when he saw the baby reach for his rattle with his left hand. So, John stuffed the baby's tiny hand into a tobacco sack and tied the drawstring around the baby's wrist. There his son's hand stayed until John King was satisfied he was going to be a right-hander, after all.

Once when he was playing for Galveston, King drove in two runs with a double early in the game. But when the opposition sent in a lefty reliever, King was replaced by a pinch-hitter. In anger, he ran to the scoreboard in center field and pulled down the two-run marker and returned to the dugout.

He told his astonished manager, "If I can't bat, you can't have my two runs."

While playing for Lubbock, King and some of his teammates were walking down the street when they came to a blind violinist who was begging on a corner. King deposited a coin in the tin cup and the man began playing a tune. When King saw he was a left-hander, he promptly went back and snatched the coin from the cup, muttering about left-handers.

King spent all of his time in the minors. He later became an umpire in the Cotton States and Texas leagues, retiring in 1932. Oil was discovered on his property and he became a millionaire and moved to Lubbock.

At the age of 86, John King died in Kilgore, Texas in 1976. He had moved back to Kilgore, he said, because in Lubbock he had too many left-handed neighbors.

In the spring of 1974 two American League stars were nearing the end of their careers. One was Dave McNally, Baltimore's left-hand pitching ace; the other was Al Kaline, Detroit's superstar outfielder, who was zeroing in on the 3,000th hit of his career. Although they knew each other as competitors, they were not close friends.

One spring day, the phone rang in Al Kaline's Bloomfield Hills, Michigan home. It was Dave McNally.

"Al," he said, "I'm trying to get a Ford dealership here in the Billings, Montana area. Do you know anybody at Ford?"

"Sure," said Kaline. "I know the president, Lee Iacocca."

"Can you call him for me?" asked McNally.

Kaline agreed and phoned his friend Iacocca. Iacocca, a baseball fan, knew about McNally and told Al, "I'll do what I can."

By the middle of the '74 baseball season, McNally had his Ford agency. Again, he phoned Kaline: "Al, I just want to thank you for your help with Iacocca. I'm all set here, and I couldn't have done it without you.

"By the way, maybe because you were on my mind, I had a dream about you last night. I dreamed that you got your 3,000th hit off me."

Fast-forward another month to September 1974. In Baltimore's Memorial Stadium, Dave McNally is pitching; Al Kaline is at bat. Kaline swings, drives a McNally pitch into the right-field corner, and races into second.

The game is stopped and the celebration of Al Kaline's 3,000th career hit begins. Sometimes dreams do come true.

Lou Gehrig's 2,130 consecutive-games-played streak is baseball's most famous. And yet, that streak never would have begun except for a headache ... a headache that struck a man who lived many years in Lansing, Michigan—Wally Pipp.

Some 25 years ago, I did an interview for the *Sporting News* with the late Wally Pipp. I drove to Lansing and spent a very pleasant day with him. He told me the story of his famous headache ... the headache over which Pipp lost his job, a Baseball Hall-of-Famer got his start, and a fantastic streak was begun.

Wally Pipp started in the bigs as a Tiger. He hit only .161 in 12 games in 1913 and was soon in the minors. After a couple of good minor-league years, he joined the Yankees in 1915. The Tigers had still owned Wally during those minor-league seasons, but Frank Navin had a chance to sell him and he peddled Wally to the Yanks. Wally told me that Navin realized he had made a mistake with the sale: He asked Wally to refuse to report, but Wally decided to go with the New York team.

Pipp led the league in home runs during a couple of those Yankee years and became a firm fixture at first base. He had a dugout fight with another home-run hitter—Babe Ruth. They tangled in 1923 in St. Louis. The Babe had criticized Wally's play at first base, and Pipp went after the Big Guy.

Somehow fate decreed that the careers of Pipp and Lou Gehrig would intertwine. Pipp's first contact with the all-time Yankee great came when he scouted him in 1922. At that time, Wally had been with the Yankees for seven years. The owner of the Indianapolis club, William C. Smith, asked Pipp to look over young Gehrig, then playing for Columbia University. He promised Wally $500 if he could get Gehrig's name on an Indianapolis contract.

Pipp watched Gehrig in action and tried to sign him; but Lou told Wally that the Yanks and Giants were after him and that if he signed, it would be with one of those two New York clubs.

Gehrig did sign with the Yankees and was sent to the Hartford club. Then the stories of Pipp and Gehrig once again began to intertwine. Pipp sprained his ankle in September of 1923 and Gehrig was recalled from Hartford to play first base for the final weeks of the season.

For the next two years, Gehrig divided his time between New York and Hartford. Incidentally, Pipp told me that in those early Gehrig days, he and others felt that Lou would never make it in the big leagues. The Yanks had offered Gehrig in a trade to the Browns. And manager Miller Huggins told Pipp that he was about set to farm Gehrig to the American Association.

When the '25 season was two months old, Gehrig was still a bench-warmer and Pipp the first baseman. On June 1, Gehrig pinch-hit for Pee Wee Wanninger. Before the game the next afternoon, Pipp told his manager, Miller Huggins, that his head was aching.

"Try a couple of aspirin," Huggins told him. "Take the day off, and the kid can replace you."

It turned out to be some day off for Wally Pipp. He never played another game at first base for the Yankees. When the kid —Lou Gehrig—took over first base that afternoon, he stayed there. He played every Yankee game from that date, until May 2, 1939—a record streak of 2,130 games.

Pipp might have returned to action within several days. But on the afternoon he was ready to play again, he was beaned in batting practice by a rookie pitcher named Charlie Caldwell (who later won fame as a Princeton football coach). Pipp suffered a fractured skull. With Gehrig entrenched at first base, the Yankees traded Wally to Cincinnati the following winter.

On the day Gehrig stopped his streak of consecutive games, May 2, 1939, Wally Pipp had been retired from baseball for ten years. But he still figured in the Gehrig story. Wally was visiting his old Yankee teammates in Detroit that morning. He saw Gehrig, the man who had replaced him.

"I'm not feeling well, Wally," Lou told Pipp. "I might not play today."

Sure enough, that was the day Gehrig asked his manager, Joe McCarthy, to take him out of the lineup. It was the end of his record-breaking streak.

In two years Lou Gehrig was dead. His death came on June 2, 1941. It was on the same day—exactly 16 years before—that he had replaced Wally Pipp at first base for the Yankees.

And had it not been for Pipp's famous headache on that June day in 1925, the baseball story of the great Lou Gehrig might have been entirely different.

Although the pennant-winning Yankees were best known for their overall slugging prowess, over the years they could also boast of some outstanding pitchers.

And the Yankee hurler who holds most of the club pitching records was the "Chairman of the Board," Ed "Whitey" Ford. Ed holds the records for the New York club in most games, most innings pitched, most strike-outs, most victories, most shutouts and the lowest lifetime earned run average.

Also, as Whitey used to say, he led the league in luck.

This statement you can discount to a degree because of Mr. Ford's modesty, but there was one afternoon at

Yankee Stadium which could be entered as evidence that indeed Whitey Ford was blessed with an inordinate amount of luck.

As Whitey was pitching that afternoon, a piece of paper blew onto the field in front of him. After a pitch, he left the mound to pick it up. And that piece of paper was a two-dollar bill.

As they say, luck is where you find it. And that's where Ford found it—right at the mound.

He experienced one of the most profitable days in big-league history and didn't even play that afternoon.

His name was Francis James "Salty" Parker. He played only 11 games in the majors, yet his name will be forever linked with those few rookies who have had their lucky moments.

On June 20, 1936, Salty was called up from the Detroit Tigers' Toledo farm club and reported to Briggs Stadium. After the game, he was leaving the clubhouse with teammate Marv Owen. Three men approached them.

"Marv," said one of them. "You're coming tonight to our banquet, aren't you?"

"I'm not sure. But I'll try," said Owen.

"If you come, bring the kid along," said another, pointing to the rookie Salty Parker.

Owen decided to go and Parker went with him. General Motors was staging the banquet for its Chevrolet dealers. All the Tiger players had been invited. Only six came—Jack Burns, Schoolboy Rowe, Goose Goslin, and Gee Walker, in addition to Owen and Parker. After a few speeches, Walker started to leave.

"Wait a minute," the emcee, a Mr. Haller, said. "Don't go yet, Gee. We at GM are here tonight to prove to Detroit and Michigan that we are a hundred percent behind the Tigers. We are going to present each of you who came here tonight with a brand new 1936 Chevrolet."

Salty Parker couldn't believe his ears. Here he was in his first day in the big leagues—he hadn't even played a game—and he was going to get a free Chevrolet. The other players—all veterans—congratulated each other on their wisdom in attending the banquet. The next day, it was a different story for the 19 Tigers who had skipped the party. They didn't get automobiles.

Many moaned that they had followed the long-established baseball precept: Never attend a banquet if you can possibly get out of it.

"I had a cousin come to town and I had to see him," said one veteran. "So I missed the banquet. I hope he goes to h--- and I never see him again."

A reporter asked Charlie Gehringer why he didn't go. "I wouldn't go to that banquet or any other—even if the Pope had asked me," he replied.

Salty Parker didn't make his big-league debut until ten days later. He had time to worry about whether he was really going to get a new car or not. The Chevy people had asked each player for his color preference, and that had caused the delay. Finally, six happy Tigers went to a dealer and picked up their cars.

Salty played in only 11 games for the Tigers ... and that was the extent of his big-league career. Later, he coached in the big leagues and was an interim manager for both Houston and the Mets. But baseball will remember Salty Parker as the rookie who got a free car on his first day in the big leagues ... for being at a banquet many of his teammates refused to attend.

Jimmy Ring, who pitched for the Phils and the Reds, batted with a fielder's glove in his hip pocket. He thought it was good luck.

Clark Griffith, pitching for the White Sox, thought it was bad luck to pitch a shutout. He would beg his teammates to let the opposing team score so bad luck wouldn't haunt him.

Bill Armour, Detroit manager in 1905–06 was superstitious about butterflies. If he saw one, he'd order the players to stop the game, chase it and kill it. If they failed, he believed his team would never win.

In 1905 in Salt Lake City, William Griffiths was playing first base for an amateur team. A grounder hit a pebble and went over his head. Disgusted, he looked at the pebble, examined it later and found it was a gold nugget. He went back that night, picked up some other pebbles and contacted some friends. Griffiths bought the ballpark, dug a mine, and became a millionaire.

Joe Dugan, the old Yankee, would never throw the ball to the pitcher unless for a putout. Babe Ruth used to touch second base on the way to the outfield. Eddie Collins would take his gum out and put it on his cap when there were two strikes on him. Minnie Minoso showered in a complete uniform one time to wash away a jinx. Hugh Casey would have no pictures taken before the game. Jackie Robinson always walked in front of the catcher, not behind the catcher and the umpire.

Hall-of-Famer Bob Feller remembers that Oscar Vitt— his old manager—picked his starting pitchers in a crazy way. Vitt's wife was an astrology buff and relayed information she found in the stars to her husband. The pitcher of the day got the word when he found the baseball under his uniform cap.

Good eyesight may be a requisite for top-notch leadoff men. Davy Jones of the Tigers in the early American League attributed his fine eyesight to the fact that before bedtime he always ate Limburger cheese on rye and drank two bottles of beer.

ELEVEN

Trailblazers

"I try not to break the rules, but merely to test their elasticity."

Bill Veeck

There is usually a set pattern in the way baseball rules undergo change. First, there's a rule; then a player figures a way to circumvent it; and finally the rule has to be discarded or changed.

Take the case of Tommy McCarthy and the base runner advancing on a fly ball. When McCarthy played outfield in the 1890s for the Boston Braves, a runner was not allowed to tag a base and leave until the fielder had held a fly ball and was ready to throw it.

So, Mr. McCarthy came up with a trick. He would juggle the ball before he caught it, and as he was juggling, he would run toward the infield. Under the rule, the runner had to stick to his base until Tommy actually held the ball. So, the runner could never advance after a fly under those conditions.

McCarthy's trick made a shambles of the rule, so it was changed. Now, the runner can tag and advance on a caught fly as soon as the ball touches the glove of the fielder.

One of the true adventurers in baseball's march of progress had to be the first catcher brave enough to crawl up right behind the batter.

Until 1866 all catchers by custom and habit stood about 50 feet behind the batter and caught pitches on the first bounce. Certainly it was a safe way, even if not the most effective.

But then along came a bold man named Nat Hicks. Nat became the first to get close behind the batter—without a mask, shin guards, chest protector or even a mitt. Nat was a real pioneer among baseball backstops.

Later, Hicks caught for the New York Mutuals and was with that club when Art Cummings, the inventor of the curve ball, pitched for them.

As baseball progressed, catchers began to get more protection with the mitt, mask, shin guards and other paraphernalia. But old Nat Hicks was behind the bat all by himself.

It is generally agreed by the historians of baseball that shin guards were introduced to the game by Roger Bresnahan, Hall-of-Fame catcher for the New York Giants, just after the turn of the century.

And they're right ... up to a point. Bresnahan was the first to wear his shin guards on the outside of his uniform. But prior to that, two players had worn shin guards under their stockings. One was Harry Steinfeldt, a Cincinnati third baseman; and the other was the old Philadelphia Phils catcher Charles "Red" Dooin.

Bresnahan came up with his innovation, independent

of the other two, by the way, from watching a goaltender in a roller polo rink in 1908. When he first wore his shin guards he was teased and taunted about them. But only a few years later no decent catcher would be "caught" without a pair.

In turn-of-the-century baseball, fouls did not count as strikes, as they do today.

Then along came a young collegian named Roy Thomas to join the Philadelphia Phils. Thomas was very adept at fouling off pitches. Other smart hitters of that day could do the same thing to wear down a pitcher, but Thomas was probably the best of all. One afternoon he fouled off 25 straight pitches from Brooklyn pitcher Bill "Brickyard" Kennedy. This didn't make Mr. Kennedy very happy. He was wearing out his arm and had nothing to show for all that effort. It made Kennedy's manager, Ned Hanlon, even madder.

Hanlon shouted to Thomas, "All right, you might get away right now with fouling off those pitches, but we'll take care of you this coming winter."

And, so he did. During the winter Hanlon helped push through a new National League rule: If a batter fouls off a pitch at any time except with two strikes on him, it will be ruled as a strike.

You know that old expression: "You can't steal first base." Well now you can't, but way back in Tiger history a man did. In fact, he made a habit of it, and caused a change in baseball's rules.

Who was he? The great clown Germany Schaefer, second baseman for Detroit on those pennant-winning teams of 1907, '08, and '09.

One day against Cleveland, Schaefer was on first and Davy Jones on third. The sign was given for the double-steal. Germany was on his way about the time the young rookie pitcher let the ball go. He reached second almost before the catcher, Nig Clarke, had the ball. Jones stayed at third.

Then Schaefer, on second, yelled to Jones at third. "Hey! We'll try it again." He dashed back toward first base and made it safely. Such a crazy move upset the pitcher: He held the ball in amazement and Jones, the runner on third, raced across home plate. Then Schaefer ran to second again. For the rest of the year Schaefer claimed that the scorer should have given him three stolen bases: second, first and then second again.

In any case, Germany Schaefer was the last man to steal first base. That winter the rules-makers got together and passed the rule that now prohibits any runner from running the bases in reverse.

Uniforms have always fascinated people. I've worn a few in my lifetime, the first when I was in the ROTC in high school in Atlanta. The military hadn't changed any styles since World War I, and I wore those hot and scratchy wool flannel khakis. In the Marines (and I was in for four years) we wore blues on formal occasions—wool again, with a high tight collar. For other occasions we had cotton khakis or dungarees.

I liked the dungarees best: They were comfortable. The others weren't bad, except I always had to spend a lot of time starching and ironing my shirts—Marines were big on spit and polish.

I haven't worn any kind of a uniform in years ... and I hope I don't have to. But my most vivid memories of uniforms are my old baseball suits.

In sandlot days when I played ball, nobody had a uniform. We had spikes, sometimes, and a glove. Other than that, you played in what you wore all the time—a pair of slacks and a sport shirt.

Even in American Legion baseball, I wore no uniform. My team played in the city finals, but in those Depression days nobody had enough money to outfit a team. You wore what you had.

There was one exception in my boyhood. A pair of old Georgia Tech football players, Everett Strupper and Pup Phillips, were in the insurance business and they came up with a unique idea. They started a kids baseball league. In return, parents had to buy life insurance on the kids. The league was made up of six teams in different sections of Atlanta. Each team had a cheap little cotton uniform. I was on the Terrors, and I was really proud of that uniform.

A year or two later I got to know an old semi-pro ballplayer named Blackie Blackstock. He knew some of the Atlanta Cracker players and got me an old, discarded Cracker uniform. This one was my real pride. I wore it around the house and often played sandlot ball in it.

The uniform was pin-striped—dark blue stripes on white. It was about five sizes too big for me. Its weight dragged me down and when it was wet it weighed even more. It was made of heavy wool—hot, scratchy, heavy wool. I was terribly uncomfortable in that old uniform, but I wore it anyway.

And there was something else about uniforms back in the '30s. A ballplayer—pro or amateur—had to learn to put one on. You turned the pants inside out, then put your legs through the leg holes, instead of through the waist. You drew the pants over your legs and then fastened the bottom of the uniform legs with a rubber band. Complicated and uncomfortable they may have been, but we were proud to wear them.

Switch hitters have always fascinated baseball fans. Bob Ferguson of the old Brooklyn Atlantics was the first. And

Bob became a switch hitter one afternoon—June 14 to be exact—in 1870.

George Wright, the shortstop for the Cincinnati Redlegs was getting all the chances off the bats of the Atlantics. And George was the star player of his time. So in an effort to keep the ball away from George Wright, Bob Ferguson, a natural right-hand batter, switched to the left-hand side of the plate. Thus he became the game's first switch hitter.

Over the years, outstanding switch hitters have included Mickey Mantle, Pete Rose, Rip Collins, Frank Frisch, Dave Bancroft, Max Carey and Lu Blue. Mantle leads the others in lifetime home runs by a great margin, hitting a total of 536 in his brilliant career with the New York Yankees.

In modern baseball, pinch-hitting is a way of life. The man who can come off the bench and deliver the big hit to win a game can command star status and a big salary. But nobody in early baseball had ever heard of pinch-hitting. In fact, it was not until 1891 that the rules even allowed such maneuvering, and then not until the next season that the first pinch-hitter actually appeared.

Pat Tebeau, playing manager of the old Cleveland team, was the first manager to use a pinch-hitter. On June 7, 1892, in Brooklyn he sent in Jack Doyle to bat for the Cleveland pitcher, George Davies. Doyle came through ... he singled. During that 1892 season, only seven substitute batters were used all season long in the entire National League. Nowadays, you may occasionally see that many pinch-hitters used in one game.

The DH—designated hitter—rule has been around since 1973 when the American League adopted it for three years on an experimental basis. In 1975, the league decided to make the rule permanent, although the National League still opposes its use. The irony of the rule is that it was first proposed by National League President John Heydler more than 60 years ago.

Heydler had a deep background in baseball. After quitting his job as a linotype operator in Washington, D.C., he served the National League in almost every capacity. He was an umpire, statistician, secretary to the president, secretary of the league and, finally, the president from 1918 to 1934.

Heydler was an ardent Republican and a most conservative man—in politics, in his league administration and in his personal life. Yet, in 1929 he advanced a radical idea to baseball.

Heydler talked over his idea with longtime friend Fred Lieb, the distinguished baseball writer. Fred told him that he thought the idea had merit and he should propose it. A couple of weeks later, Heydler released his plan to the country via radio and the press associations.

Here was his rationale: "My thought in offering this rule change is to make baseball a better and livelier game. As far back as my years as a National League umpire, I used to think that one of the dullest things in baseball was a team having a good batting rally stopped by the pitcher coming up to strike out."

Fans all over the country reacted violently against the plan. Two National League executives—John McGraw and Wilbert Robinson—supported the DH plan, but not with much enthusiasm. The other club executives were cool to it or indifferent.

However, it was in the American League that the DH plan met its stiffest opposition. The American League called it "damfoolery" and tried to laugh it off the sports pages. "It's silly, it's stupid," one American Leaguer said. "We are surprised that a man like John Heydler would sponsor it. We have a great game. Let's keep it that way.

Nine players make up a baseball team just as sure as 12 eggs make a dozen."

In the winter meetings the idea of the DH never came up. Even McGraw, one of its supporters, kept silent. It died aborning, so to speak.

For many years, nobody thought about the DH. Then in 1973 it resurfaced. Its champion was again a league president—but this time the boss of the American League, Joe Cronin.

Like Heydler, Cronin had been in all phases of baseball, but he was best known as a player, a fine shortstop. And it might have been Joe's success as a manager/pinch-hitter that prompted him to sponsor the DH proposal. During the World War II player shortage in 1943, Cronin set a record of five consecutive home runs for a pinch-hitter. Four of those home runs came with two men on base. Cronin couldn't run in those final days of his career and his strong arm was gone, but he could still hit.

So, Cronin used his weight as the American League president and the league adopted the DH rule. It was temporary at first, but after two years of experimentation, the league made the rule permanent. Like it or not, it's now a part of baseball.

And somewhere old John Heydler, the National League president, must be chuckling. John suggested the rule change in 1929, and they laughed at him. And then 44 years later the rival league came around to make it a reality.

The first truly one-handed catcher may have been Bruce Edwards of Brooklyn. Back in the 1940s, Bruce hurt his throwing hand and had to keep it behind his back. Later, Randy Hundley of Chicago was credited by many to be the first one-handed catcher. Johnny Bench, of course, brought it to its ultimate.

Bat racks were introduced in 1935 by the Cub groundskeeper at Wrigley Field, Bobby Doerr. Bobby was worried when he saw the Cub third baseman, Stan Hack, trip over bats several times. Also, he wanted to find a way to keep the bats from getting damp.

Platooning goes back at least as far as May 20, 1881. This is from the *Buffalo Express:* "Manager [Jim] O'Rourke will lay off [Deacon] White today because a left-hander, [Lee] Richmond, is pitching for Worcester."

Why is "K" used to designate a strikeout? In the 1850s, statistician Henry Chadwick said that the last letter of each word describing a play would be used in the scoring. He put "D" for ball caught on the first bound, "L" for foul, and "K" for struck. Of those, only "K" survives.

Ron Blomberg of the New York Yankees was the first designated hitter to appear in a regular-season game. He was walked by Luis Tiant of the Boston Red Sox in the top of the first inning April 6, 1973.

Ushers appeared in New York baseball parks in 1912 after Ty Cobb had gone into the stands to fight a heckler.

It's a myth that the Yankees went to pinstripes to offset the portly appearance of Babe Ruth when he joined them in 1920. The truth is the Yankees first wore pinstripes in 1912. And that was the first year they were officially known as the Yankees.

At the start of an inning, a pitcher is allowed eight warm-ups in one minute. Before 1911, the rule didn't exist: The pitcher simply got a few tosses. During a game between the A's and the Red Sox, the A's Stuffy McInnis came to the plate to lead off. When Ed Karger threw a practice toss, McInnis hit it into the empty outfield and circled the bases for a home run. After that, they made the new rule.

Babe Ruth just missed the night-ball era. Ruth retired from the Boston Braves June 2, 1935, a week after the Reds and Phils had played the first night game in Cincinnati.

The hit and run was developed by Ned Hanlon in Baltimore in 1894. Thirteen times in a row Baltimore used the maneuver against New York, which caused manager John Montgomery Ward to protest that the Baltimore team was playing a new game and not baseball.

The system of having umpires assigned by leagues originated with William A. Hulbert, the second president of the National League. Up until his time, the team captains picked their own umpires. Hulbert also standardized the price of admission at 50 cents.

Before 1893, the distance from home plate to the pitcher's slab was 50 feet. It's been said that Amos Rusie, the New York fireballer, threw so hard that the slab was moved back to protect batters from his blinding speed. Instead, it gave Rusie's curve a chance to break, and he was an even better pitcher.

Connie Mack, the Hall-of-Fame manager, originated battery signs in 1888. He was catching at that time for Washington.

The first batting helmet may have been worn by Jackie Hayes, the White Sox second baseman who was blind in his right eye. In 1940, the Sox fashioned a homemade helmet that fit over the top of his head and covered his ears.

The fork ball is really the split finger of today, and the inventor is Joe Bush, who pitched for the A's, the Yankees, the Red Sox, the Browns, Washington, the Giants and Pittsburgh. In 1920, Joe Bush picked up a ball in batting practice, inserted it between his index and middle finger and threw it. It hit the Boston catcher, Al Walters, in the chest. The next one hit him on the knee, and then he began to use it as a pitch.

Bill Veeck was not the first of the baseball promoters. In St. Louis in the 1890s Chris von Der Ahe—in the pregame festivities—would have horse racing, Wild West shows, shoot the shoots and an all-girl band. He put red stockings on his players, who eventually became the Cardinals. And, some people think he coined the term "fan" from fanatic.

Before 1869, foul lines were made by digging furrows with a plow. That year, the Cincinnati groundskeeper, Will Weed, was the first to make lines with chalk.

George Cuppy, who used to pitch for the Cleveland Spiders in the National League, is best remembered as one of the slowest pitchers in the game. But he also introduced the National League practice of the pitchers wearing fielding gloves.

Ernie Quigley, the National League umpire, was working a game between Boston and Brooklyn in 1912 or '13 when Earl Yingling was pitching, and Yingling dropped the ball as he wound up. There was no rule to cover this play. After the game, Quigley went to Tom Lynch, president of the league. What if the pitcher should drop the ball with three runners in motion? He could pick it right up and have a play at any base. Lynch then introduced the rule which makes such an action a balk.

A pitcher named Wilbert Hubbell of the Phillies twice walked a man on purpose by throwing four pitches to first base, not home plate. After the second time, the league president, John Heydler, warned him that he'd be suspended if he did it again. The rules were then revised to prevent such action.

TWELVE

A Man's Got to Make a Livin'

"He had both players and money—and just didn't like to
see the two of them mix."
                    Chuck Conners (on owner Branch Rickey)

The contract holdout is as old as professional baseball. The first pro team in history—the 1869
Cincinnati Red Stockings—had a holdout. Charles
Sweasy in 1870 wanted $1,000 a year, an increase of $200,
but he didn't get it.

Many others have followed old Charlie's lead. And,
there have been cases—only a few—of players sitting
out entire seasons, rather then signing at terms that they
thought were too low.

Perhaps one of the strangest holdouts was that of Ossee Schreckengost, a catcher on one of Connie Mack's
Philadelphia Athletic teams in the early 1900s. In those
days roommates not only roomed together, but they slept
in the same bed.

Now, Ossee's roommate was one of the most eccentric
characters in baseball history—Rube Waddell.

Compared to Rube, old Dizzy Dean was as calm and sedate as a college professor. Waddell had many screwball tendencies. One of those was his fondness for animal crackers, or more especially, his fondness for eating those animal crackers in bed. And that's where Schreckengost and his holdout came in.

Schreckengost told his manager, Connie Mack, that he wouldn't sign a contract, no sir, not unless he put a clause in there that Waddell couldn't eat crackers in bed.

Well, Connie Mack agreed ... Ossee Schreckengost signed ... and Rube Waddell had to eat his animal crackers someplace else.

World Series players' shares are the same for four games as they are for five, six, or even seven. But it wasn't always that way. Things changed back in the Series of 1907 between Detroit and the Chicago Cubs. In those days of long spikes and short tempers, baseball was ruled by the National Commission, a sort of three-man Fay Vincent. The commission consisted of Garry Herrmann, the well-upholstered owner of the Reds (he was chairman), and Ban Johnson and Harry Pulliam, the presidents of the two majors.

The afternoon before the Series was to open, the commission held a special meeting to give players, managers, owners and umpires final instructions. After several weary hours, chairman Herrmann rapped the gavel and asked: "Has any player a question before the meeting's adjourned?"

A knotty hand went up. It belonged to Germany Schaefer, Detroit second baseman and one of the early-day clowns of baseball.

Schaefer was saying: "Yes, I have an important question." Already the mob was grinning. Schaefer had some joke up his sleeve ... they knew it. He was a card. A bit irked, the chairman replied: "Yes, Schaefer, there are nine men on a side. And over the fence is not out. Anything else?"

Schaefer held his ground and asked his question: "Is a tie game a legal game?"

Chairman Herrmann snapped: "Of course not. A tie is not a legal game and must be played over. Why ask such a question?"

By now the crowd was laughing and Schaefer had to shout his answer: "Well, the rules say the players share the gate receipts for only the first four games. Does that mean that if we have a tie, we share the receipts for the first five?"

The chairman was peeved. He pontificated. "There is no chance whatsoever for a tie in the World Series."

But second baseman Schaefer still wasn't satisfied, and he wanted a ruling.

"All right," chairman Herrmann shouted, "you'll get a ruling. A tie is not a game. Therefore, in case of a tie in the first four games, the players will be awarded gate receipts paid for the first five games."

That night, all around the Loop in Chicago, it was a big joke. That clowning Dutchman Schaefer (they said) was a funny one. Imagine the players getting five gate receipts. Imagine a tie in the World Series.

The meeting was a big story in the morning papers and fans were still laughing about it at the first game that afternoon. In that battle, the Tigers led 3–1 going into the ninth. The Cubs scored one and had runners on second and third with two out. With two strikes on pinch-hitter Del Howard, Wild Bill Donovan threw a perfect curve. It broke across and Howard swung and missed. But Charlie "Boss" Schmidt, the Detroit catcher, let the pitch get away to the crowd and the score was tied.

Into extra innings they went, fighting each other and the darkness, too. In the 12th, Chicago began to rally. With one out and Jimmy Sheckard on, Frank Chance banged a hard liner over second. Then out of those shadows came Germany Schaefer. He pulled the drive down, somehow, and Sheckard, already almost to second, was doubled off first. The umps called it for darkness right there ... a 3–3 tie.

There was talk next day about the meeting ... about the third strike getting away from Schmidt to tie the game ... about Schaefer's great catch to keep it tied.

So, that winter, the National Commission passed a new rule: no more of this tie-game nonsense. Henceforth, the first four gates would be shared by the players—tie or no tie.

And Germany Schaefer swore 'til his dying day that he had seen it all in a dream a week before the Series, and that was why he'd asked Garry Herrmann and the National Commission whether a tie constituted a legal game or not.

The year was 1918 ... World War I was on. But the major leaguers kept playing. Because of the war, the season was a dismal one and was cut short: It ended on Labor Day.

The Cubs and the Red Sox met in a hurriedly planned World Series. But the players weren't happy. For the first time, the pennant winners had to divide their World Series shares with other first-division teams.

Attendance was poor for the first four games, so there was little money to share. And just before the fifth game in Boston, the players decided they'd strike—more money or we don't play.

Enter the three-man National Commission. And the strong man of that commission was Ban Johnson, the iron-willed president of the American League. It looked as if it would fall to Johnson to stop the strike.

But Ban Johnson didn't even know about the strike: He'd been drinking in a Boston bar all morning, and he was drunk.

He got to the ballpark late, found the stands full of fans, but no players on the field. He quickly met with the two teams' player representatives—Les Mann of the Cubs and Harry Hooper of the Red Sox.

The mood was ugly. The players refused to play, America was at war, the public had little interest in baseball. But the players were thinking of only one thing—more money. A wrong move here could not only put an end to the World Series, but it could cause a lasting scandal.

And the big boss of baseball was drunk.

Johnson tried to pull himself together, assuming an air of judicial dignity. He turned to Hooper: "Harry, do you know what you will do to baseball's good name if you don't play?"

Before the player could answer, Johnson flung his arm around Hooper's shoulder. "Go out there," he pleaded, "your fans are waiting."

Hooper looked at Mann. The two players shrugged their shoulders. It was plain that Johnson was in no condition to discuss anything. So, the two teams took the field. The Series went on and scandal was avoided.

If Johnson had been sober and able to talk, there might have been a bitter confrontation. A strike. Instead, baseball was saved because its most important man had too much to drink.

A clipping from the July 1, 1985 *Sporting News* announced the death of a former American League pitcher named Johnny Broaca. Part of the item caught my eye. In 1937 Broaca was pitching for the Yankees. When they beat the Giants in the World Series, the Yankees did not vote Broaca a $6,000 share, but they voted his wife a partial share of $1,000. It has to be the only time in history that a player's wife got his winning share—and not the player.

But there are many other strange twists to the career

of John Broaca. Let's begin with some basic facts. He was born in 1909 in Lawrence, Massachusetts. He attended Yale, where he was a standout pitcher. He pitched five years in the big leagues—four with the Yankees and one with Cleveland. Broaca's best year was his second season with New York, when he won 15 and lost 7. That was 1935. And, he was one of the few players of his time who wore glasses.

When Broaca went to Yale, he worked his way through school, waiting on tables and doing odd jobs on the campus. He spent less than a year in the minors before joining the Yankees in 1934. Johnny broke into the majors with a bang. He pitched a three-hitter and a one-hitter in his first two starts. In 1936 he was pitching well, but with no explanation he left his team in mid-season. He did the same thing the next year—still unexplained.

He was with the Yankees when they beat the Giants in the 1936 World Series. He was on the eligible list, but never got to pitch. He was not around at all for the '37 Series. There were stories that he planned to pursue a career in professional boxing, and also talk that he was having trouble with his marriage. Anyway, the Yankees put Broaca on the suspended list.

The sportswriter Damon Runyon called Broaca "the first fugitive from a World Series."

Johnny Broaca never pitched again for the Yankees. He remained on the suspended list in 1938. He tried professional boxing briefly, but never won a fight. In 1939 he surfaced again, this time with the Cleveland Indians. He made 22 appearances, all but two in relief. His seasonal record was four wins and two losses.

After that he drifted away. And little was heard about Broaca until the obit notice in the *Sporting News*. He died May 16, 1985, in the same town where he was born, Lawrence, Massachusetts.

We do know that John Broaca's wife was the only wife ever to be awarded a World Series share; but there are still many mysteries about Broaca himself, a pitcher who was a strange footnote in baseball history.

In baseball, the term "money player" has two meanings: one, a player can be paid a lot; or, two, a player can come through in the clutch. Rube Marquard—a real money player of another era —filled both bills.

This story happened when Rube was only 18. It was 1908, Marquard's second season in pro ball. He pitched that year at Indianapolis, turning in 47 complete games and winning 28.

Late in the year, Indianapolis was playing at Columbus. Rube's manager, Charlie Carr, approached him before the game. He told him that both major leagues had an off day that afternoon and several big-league representatives were coming to see him pitch.

"If you pitch a good game," the manager said, "I'll be able to sell you for a good price."

So, there was money on the line—a clutch game. Rube went out that afternoon and pitched a perfect game. He faced only 27 Columbus batters: not a man reached base.

That night in Columbus, Rube was put on the auction block—up for open bidding by the big leaguers. The bidding was spirited. Cleveland, Rube's hometown, went as high as $10,500, but the New York Giants won out when they offered $11,000 for the young left-hander.

That doesn't sound like much money for a pitcher these days, but at that time it was a record price. In September, Marquard reported to the Giants, becoming a big leaguer at the age of 18.

For two years the Giants regretted they had paid such a high price. Marquard was a flop; so much a flop that the sportswriters called him "the $11,000 Lemon." But he showed them in 1911: He won 24 games that season and established himself as a top star.

Rube went on to pitch for 18 years—all of them in the

National League. He pitched for New York, Brooklyn, Cincinnati and Boston, winning a total of 201 games in his career. In 1971 he was named to the Baseball Hall of Fame.

Here was truly a money player. The $11,000 price tag in 1908 symbolized the growing professionalism of baseball in that day. And the perfect game that Rube pitched to achieve that price tag certainly proved that he was a money player in the clutch.

When I broadcast the Giant games in the 1950s, I was an avid collector. I contacted a lady named Ruth Frymir who ran a New Haven bookstore. It seems somebody had cleaned out the Yankee offices and discarded hundreds of old Yankee cancelled checks and player contracts. I bought from Miss Frymir a check made out to Babe Ruth and a contract which had belonged to Johnny Suggs, a pitcher with the Yankees in 1922 and the father of the professional golfer, Louise Suggs.

The Babe Ruth check is dated May 31, 1922, and made out to G.H. Ruth for $4,398.66. The check is drawn on the Yorkville Bank, 1511 Third Avenue, New York, and signed by Jacob Ruppert, president of the Yankees.

But the story behind the check is on the reverse side. Listed there is: "Fine by President Johnson, $200.00." And below is the Babe's endorsement.

Here's how the fine came about. Ruth had been fined and suspended by Commissioner Judge Kenesaw Mountain Landis for barnstorming (against Landis' orders) following the 1921 World Series. He missed the first six weeks of the 1922 American League season. He came back to the Yankee lineup but within a week was in trouble again. It started when umpire George Hildebrand ruled the Babe out on a close play at second base.

The Babe jumped up in a rage and began to abuse the

umpire with his choicest insults. Finally, the umpire could take no more.

"You're out of the game," he shouted at the Babe.

In those days the Yankees were playing their home games at the Polo Grounds (as they waited for the completion of Yankee Stadium). As Ruth walked off the field and headed toward the New York dugout, a loud-mouthed fan near the dugout began to berate him. The fan had been relaxing and had taken off his shoes, but he jumped to his stockinged feet and shouted obscenities toward Ruth.

Already disgusted with himself and umpire Hildebrand, Ruth was in no mood to hear any more abuse. He jumped over the box-seat railing and reached for the fan. The heckler, however, was too quick. He saw Babe coming and, still in his stockinged feet, headed for the Polo Grounds exit.

But here came the Babe right after him. The chase continued. The fan raced through the stands and out of the park, with the Babe on his heels. Finally, the fan ran all the way to the subway and disappeared down its entrance. Ruth walked slowly back to the stands and the New York clubhouse.

The fan had left his shoes at his seat but Ruth was left with nothing to show for the hectic chase—nothing but the deduction of $200 from a paycheck that later became my souvenir.

In 1928 any scout who bought a .245-hitting minor-league shortstop for $7,500 was crazy.

And that's exactly what Clark Griffith told his scout, Joe Engel, when Engel brought a skinny kid named Joe Cronin into the Washington Senators' office.

Some seven years later scout Joe Engel told Mr. Griffith that $250,000 was a lot of money. It was, and that was the price that Griff got from Boston for Joe Cronin.

Cronin had become a great star, managed the Senators to a pennant, married Griff's daughter, and then was sold in the biggest cash deal in baseball history.

At Boston he continued to star, managed the Red Sox to a pennant, and became general manager of the club. In 1956 he was named to the Baseball Hall of Fame, and later became president of the American League.

Joe Cronin was born in San Francisco only a few months after the famous earthquake—a quake that left the Cronin family with only an old rocking chair. By hard work and determination, Joe made himself one of baseball's greatest clutch hitters—and a great investment.

Baseball free agents aren't really news anymore. They're floating around all over the place, collecting their big money.

But when Rick Ferrell came along more than 60 years ago and became a free agent, he was a rarity. In fact, Rick thinks he might have been the first. If not the first, he certainly was the most unlikely.

Ferrell was a 23-year-old minor-league catcher, not too long off a North Carolina dairy farm. And he was toiling in a baseball world fraught with conservatism. No rookie ever dared speak out to challenge the establishment in those times. The average player signed whatever paper that was put in front of him and 'yes sir'ed his way through the rest of his baseball career.

But young Rick Ferrell didn't do it that way. He had thoroughly studied his contract, and during the season of 1928 he began to realize that he was being covered up by his employers, the Detroit Tigers.

Detroit had signed Rick in 1926 and first assigned him to Kinston in his native state. By 1928 he was in his third year as a Tiger farmhand and had been sent to Columbus, Ohio to work for owner Joe Carr.

"Keep this youngster a year for me," Tiger owner Frank Navin had told Carr. "At the end of the year I'll send you $5,000 for your trouble." No agreement, no papers. Baseball was so much more informal then.

By mid-season, Rick Ferrell was batting .380, but was getting nothing from anybody—only promises. The Columbus team had an off-day in Toledo and Rick decided to call on Tiger owner Frank Navin.

"I took a bus to Detroit," he recalled, "and I asked what kind of plans he had for me. He told me that should I continue to have a good year, he'd bring me up at the end of the season. It was just another promise, so I next paid a visit to Cincinnati, the parent club for Columbus. Again, only promises."

After the season ended he went to Chicago, unannounced and without an appointment, to call on Commissioner Judge Kenesaw Mountain Landis.

"I waited around for a day or two and finally got to see the commissioner's assistant, Leslie O'Connor. He heard my story, and told me to put it in writing."

Rick went home and wrote his letter. In November he was summoned to a hearing by the commissioner. Representatives of the Tigers, Redbirds and Reds also attended, as well as E.J. Hickey, president of the American Association. The rookie catcher stated his case before the high ruler of baseball and the other veteran executives.

He must have made an excellent plea, because commissioner Landis freed Ferrell from all contractual obligations and told him to put himself on the market for open bids. He became, he thinks, baseball's first free agent.

Several clubs contacted Rick immediately. John McGraw, Giant manager, was calling constantly. But Browns' owner Phil Ball (probably on a tip from his personal friend Navin) sent Bill Friel to North Carolina to sign Ferrell for the St. Louis club.

Friel camped on Rick's doorstep and finally signed him

for a bonus of $25,000 and a three-year contract at $10,000 per year. All of this came at a time when very few big-league stars were even approaching the $10,000 per year mark.

For Rick it was the beginning of a long and illustrious baseball career—18 years as a catcher in the majors, then more than 30 years as a coach, scout and executive for the Tigers. It was quite a move in those reactionary days of baseball when the 23-year-old rookie challenged the establishment, won and became baseball's first free agent.

"Very charming, very bright and very pleasant to do business with." That was a quote from John McHale, president of the Montreal Expos. The agent he was talking about was the agent for Manny Trillo. Her name? Mrs. Manny Trillo.

"How much of a cut did she get from her client?" somebody asked her. Her reply: "I get all of it."

Back in the 1950s, when Frank Lane was the general manager of the White Sox, he had a Cuban pitcher named Sandy Consuegra. Sandy didn't bother to learn English, so when Mr. Lane talked contract with him over the phone, Sandy let his 12-year-old son do all his negotiating for him.

One day, when pitcher Cy Seymour was not in the New York lineup, he was assigned to tend a turnstile; that was a common practice in the 1890s. Later, when he left his post to check on the progress of the game, his absence was discovered and he was fined $10.

Ernie Diehl, shortstop for Pittsburgh in 1903–04 and Boston in 1906–07, refused to take pay. He was later a Cincinnati councilman and a social lion in Cincinnati.

The first real giveaway day in modern baseball was Bat Day with the St. Louis Browns in 1952. The business manager of the Browns bought 12,000 bats at a close-out sale and gave them away at a double-header, which drew 15,000 fans.

In 1922, Max Carey stole 51 bases in 53 tries. Max's top salary was $16,000. He made that after he hit .343 in 1925.

Joe Engel was the owner and president of the Chattanooga Lookouts. One of his hold-out players wired Engel, "Double my salary or count me out." Joe's answer was this telegram: "1–2–3–4–5–6–7–8–9–10."

Harry Heilmann signed with Portland, in the Coast league, for $275 a month. "Money," he said, "was an unknown quantity around our house, so I decided when I was getting that kind of money I would practice a little frugality and surprise my mother by sending her the greater part of it. I pinched the pennies the first two months so I could send her $500. Imagine my surprise when I got a wire right back from her saying, 'Come home at once. You must be in bad company.'"

THIRTEEN

Pilots, Skippers and Chiefs

"Just hold them for a few innings, fellas. I'll think of something."

Charlie Dressen

The first two managers to make the Hall of Fame on their managing records alone were Connie Mack and John McGraw. They were both inducted in 1937, and it was fitting because they were really the first two widely known and publicized managers and they came along at the same time—in the early 1900s.

From the early 1900s into the '30s the two were paired. It was always Mack and McGraw whenever anybody talked about baseball leadership. Each dominated his league and each became an owner of a club, as well as manager.

Yet, there was a great contrast in the two. Connie Mack was always patrician; McGraw was combative. McGraw bullied; Mack coaxed. McGraw was profligate; Mack was austere. McGraw was forever attacking the umpires; Mack never left his dugout. McGraw had been an outstanding player and he used his playing reputation to reinforce his authority as manager; Mack was an indifferent player (hardly a star) who became a manager to make a living.

Connie Mack's real name was Cornelius McGilicuddy. He was a catcher in the old National League—never really a first stringer. His first managing job was with Pittsburgh in the 1890s, but he gained fame as the manager of the American League's Philadelphia A's. He set a remarkable major-league record for managers: 53 seasons in the big leagues.

John McGraw, with 33, is second to Mack in seasons managed. McGraw's first club was the Baltimore Orioles, but his fame came from his leadership of the fabled New York Giants, who for years dominated the National League.

Connie Mack was always "Connie" or "Mr. Mack." McGraw had two nicknames. "Little Napoleon" is on his plaque at Cooperstown. McGraw liked that one. He didn't like the other one: "Muggsy." That was the name thrown at him from rival dugouts, usually with a touch of meanness or sarcasm.

McGraw was a great strategist, as the nickname Napoleon might suggest. But he was a down-and-dirty fighter, too, which brought him the name of Muggsy. He was only 5'7", but he was tough. He had as many fights—on and off the field—as the later Billy Martin. And he put fear and trembling into his own players. They dared not challenge him: Those who did soon found themselves in another uniform.

Connie Mack was just the opposite. He was tall and lanky, at 6'1" and 170 lbs. His players loved and respected him. He hardly raised his voice, being quiet and softspoken. And yet, he got results, too. He built some great teams and managed some of the outstanding stars of the game.

Mack and McGraw were the first two great managers. Each in his own way set a standard for managers who were to come and dominate the game.

I first met Connie Mack, the great old patriarch of the A's, in 1940. It was December of that year—my first year in broadcasting. I was doing a sports show nightly on WSB in Atlanta. The national baseball convention came to Atlanta, and it was my duty to interview many of the top baseball people for my show. We set up a portable recording turntable in the lobby of the Ansley Hotel.

I talked about 12 minutes with Connie Mack. He was delightful. He recalled his great stars of the old days—Rube Waddell, Eddie Collins, Mickey Cochrane, Al Simmons and Jimmy Dykes. He told me stories about those guys and some of their antics—all the way back to the early 1900s and Waddell.

Then we got down to "modern" baseball and the memory that was so sharp for the early 1900s became fuzzy. I asked him about the 1940 season. "Who, Mr. Mack, was the outstanding rookie of the year?" "Well," he said, "I'd say that young man with the White Sox—the one who plays third and has a great arm. But I can't recall his name." He was talking about Bob Kennedy (the father of the current major-league catcher Terry Kennedy), who was beginning a fine 16-year career.

Connie Mack was 78 years old when we did that interview, and certainly could be excused for a slight lapse of memory. Age notwithstanding, he continued to manage the Athletics for another ten years, retiring from managing in 1950. He remained a forceful figure in the game until he died in 1956. Shortly before he died, I had another occasion to be with him.

This time it was an on-the-field ceremony. I was at Baltimore then, and the Orioles were staging a special day for Frank "Home Run" Baker. Baker hailed from the

Eastern Shore of Maryland and had been inducted into the Baseball Hall of Fame in 1955. The best years of Baker's 13-year major-league career had been the seven seasons he played for Connie Mack in Philadelphia. Connie had come down from Philadelphia to help pay tribute to his former star. At this time he was 93 years old. He could still move around all right, but his mental faculties were beginning to dim. The Oriole people who had appointed me as the emcee that afternoon told me to introduce Mr. Mack to the crowd, but be certain he didn't say any words over the mike.

"Just have him wave to the crowd," they told me.

Well, the ceremonies proceeded without a flaw. I introduced several dignitaries. Then I called on Home Run Baker. He made a short speech of thanks. Next, I introduced Connie Mack, expecting him to step forward and wave to the crowd. It didn't work that way. Instead, the 93-year-old Mack quickly grabbed the microphone from me. He had it before I realized what had happened. He began to talk and rambled on for a few minutes before I could as politely as possible get the mike back.

He was a great old man—managing 53 years in the big leagues. But I'll remember Connie Mack as the man who grabbed my mike and wouldn't let go.

The last time I saw Ty Cobb he told me about a man whose name was completely strange to me.

"No other baseball man did as much for me as George Leidy," the great Cobb said. "He helped me when I needed it the most and without his guidance I might have quit after one season."

If he had, baseball would never have known the fiery genius who led the American League hitters for 12 seasons—nine of them in a row—and finished a 24-year span of major-league activity with a lifetime batting average of .367.

Cobb's early career was hectic. He was only 17 years old when he left his father's Royston, Georgia farm and went to Augusta with a letter of introduction to the manager of the Augusta team, "Con" Strouthers.

Cobb already had written Strouthers, who was president as well as manager at Augusta, and received the reply that there might be a spot open for him, but he would have to pay his own expenses.

He reported on April 26, 1904 and Strouthers shoved him into the lineup opening day. Ty contributed a home run and a double, but Augusta lost to Columbia, 8–7. He made no errors afield and ran the bases with perfection.

However, the next afternoon Strouthers summoned Cobb. "We won't need you any more, lad. You're out of a job."

Cobb couldn't understand. The mystery deepened when Strouthers inserted the following advertisement in *Sporting Life:*

> *The Augusta Club is looking for a first-class short-stop and a hard-hitting outfielder. Will pay good money to good men.*
> *Address Con Strouthers, Augusta, Ga.*

Disillusioned and disgusted, the young Cobb decided to go to Anniston, Alabama in the independent Alabama-Tennessee League. Before leaving he wired his father of his plan. His dad, who had heartily disapproved Ty's entry into the professional game, wired back, "DON'T COME HOME A FAILURE."

He didn't. Cobb hit well at Anniston, batting .370 in 22 games and leading the league in hitting. To keep the home folks at Royston informed of his progress, Cobb penned news stories, extolling his deeds, to Grantland Rice, who was then sports editor of the *Atlanta Journal.*

These literary self back-pats also reached Augusta and the fans urged Strouthers to bring back the rookie he had so summarily released. So, hard-boiled Strouthers sent Cobb an offer.

The answer was quick and sure. "Not only will I not play for you at Augusta, but I'll never play for you anywhere," Cobb wrote.

Augusta continued to flounder in the lower regions of the Sally League and Strouthers finally sold the club. A new manager, Andy Roth, took charge of the team and Cobb returned. He finished out the 1904 season batting only .237 in 37 games. Under Roth, too, he was inhibited. Andy was amiable enough, but had little interest in teaching baseball fundamentals. Further, he refused to let Cobb run free on the base paths.

However, Roth was not back in 1905. In his place was a quiet, easygoing minor-league outfielder named George Leidy. Of no consequence himself in the agate type of baseball history, he was to give the game its greatest star.

Leidy was baseball wise. He knew men and he knew the fundamentals of the sport. Without hesitation he discerned the unlimited possibilities in young Cobb and went about to develop them.

Ty (some of the public prints were still calling him "Cy") was timid, super-sensitive, high-strung and nervous. He was a mere youngster among a crowd of hard-bitten, tough, rookie-hating veterans. But he had fire.

All this, Leidy saw—and he acted accordingly. He paid special attention to Cobb. He showed him a thoughtful kindness, something Cobb had grown to believe foreign to baseball. He spent hours drilling him in baseball fundamentals. He instilled in the youngster confidence. But, most of all, he fired him with a lasting ambition.

Near old Warren Park in Augusta that spring was an amusement park. Leidy invited the youngster to go there with him. It was all new to Cobb ... the strings of lights, the strident cries of the midway, the dancing girls, the raucous music. All of it stirred him.

With this background, Leidy appealed to Cobb's imagination with stories of the big leagues. "Ty," he told the youngster, "this is just a cheap sample of what you can reach—if you want to. You can play in the big leagues, live in swell hotels, ride in Pullmans, hobnob with the stage stars. Why, your name'll be in every paper in the country. You'll make thousands of dollars. You'll be famous."

Cobb was impressed—but it all seemed as unreal as the midway. "But how?" he asked.

"By practice, constant practice. By listening, observing and learning. And you can do it."

Cobb worked. He practiced mornings. He practiced before and after the games. Leidy worked with him on fundamentals—taught him how to bunt, to hit and run, to steal.

Moreover, for the first time Cobb had a manager who understood him. Leidy allowed him to use his own judgment at bat and on the base paths. Soon he began to flash the spark of genius that would reach full flame in 24 seasons of major-league stardom.

In that 1905 season, Ty—who had hit only .237 the year before—jumped into the batting leadership and stayed there. He finished at the top of the Sally League list with a .326 mark. In late August, he said goodbye to Leidy and went to Detroit. (The Tigers had bought him for $750.) He made his first appearance in a Tiger uniform on August 30, 1905, hitting a double off Jack Chesbro of the Yankees.

When he ended his career in 1928, he had collected 4,190 additional hits. Cobb set more than 90 major-league records and, of course, is generally regarded as the greatest player of all time.

However, it was George Leidy, an obscure bush-league manager, who discerned the latent qualities of baseball greatness in his young outfielder and started him on the road to stardom.

It's a rather ironic twist that a scrawny, unimposing lit-tle man was manager of the powerful New York Yankees in the 1920s.

Yes, Miller Huggins was almost a nobody—except that he was the leader of one of baseball's great teams. Hug nearly didn't even get the job because the Yankee owners didn't like the way he dressed. And all of his career, his mighty-muscled stars overshadowed and overwhelmed their manager, who was only 5'6."

One afternoon a Yankee batter, Whitey Witt, was called out on strikes by umpire Bill Guthrie. He put up an argument.

Out of the dugout came manager Miller Huggins to join in. Guthrie told Witt to leave the field. Witt wouldn't.

So, Guthrie ejected him. "All right," he said. "You're out of the game." Then Guthrie pointed to the little Yan-kee manager Miller Huggins, and he yelled to Witt again. "And when you go, take this bat boy with you."

At the close of the 1933 season Bucky Harris quit as manager of the Detroit Tigers. Detroit owner Frank Navin, on the lookout for a new manager, contacted Babe Ruth, baseball's famous slugger, then still playing out-field for the Yankees. Would he be interested in taking the job as manager of the Tigers? Ruth was keen on it . . . of course he would. Navin was happy. The Babe was the man he wanted.

Ruth, of course, knew that he could never get the Yan-kee managership—not without serving first at Ne-wark— the top Yankee farm team. Manager Joe Mc-Carthy was "in solid" with Jake Ruppert at New York and nothing could dislodge him. So Ruth went to the front-office man of the Yankees, Ed Barrow. Bushy-browed Ed told the Babe that he certainly would not stand in his way and told him to go ahead and take the Tiger job.

Then the machinery of the proposed deal began to grind. Barrow called Navin and said he could have Ruth for an easy price, plus an outfielder. They virtually closed the deal. And the Babe was ready to achieve his long-nurtured ambition of becoming a big-league manager.

Ruth, though, had a trip planned to Honolulu. He wanted to make that trip, then come back and sign his contract. Barrow advised him on the matter.

"Listen, Babe," he said, "you'd better hop on a train right now, go to Detroit and sign those papers. Don't wait ... do it now."

Still, the Babe wanted his trip, so he took it. But by the time he got back to the States, he'd read in the newspapers that Navin had signed Mickey Cochrane to manage the Tigers. The Babe was stunned: They couldn't do that to him. But they did. Navin had bought Mickey Cochrane from the Athletics and installed him as manager. It proved to be a good move. Mickey masterminded the Bengals to two straight pennants.

Ruth swallowed his disappointment and went on playing outfield for the Yankees. However, he lasted only one more season. After 1934 the New York club gave the Babe his release to enable him to join the Boston Braves. But the Boston promises never worked out. Babe quit there and ended up with Brooklyn.

There are many baseball observers who've maintained that Ruth, after all he had done to benefit baseball, should have been handed a manager's job. He asked for the Yankee job twice—once in 1929 when Miller Huggins died and once in 1930 when Bob Shawkey retired. Each time Colonel Ruppert told him he could have the Newark job or nothing. Each time the Babe refused. At one point he finally asked Larry MacPhail of the Yanks for the Newark job. But Larry figured that he owed the Babe nothing and told him so.

But the time the Babe should have had a big-league managerial post, he didn't miss the boat: He caught the boat, the boat to Honolulu, and missed the job.

A few years ago I found some newspaper clippings from the day Babe Ruth died in August of 1948. In one of those stories writer Lyall Smith recalled an interview he did with Ruth. The Babe told Smith that delaying his decision about the Tiger manager's job was the biggest "boot" of his career.

"I'm in the Hawaiian Islands, playing exhibition ball," the Babe said. "I pick up the paper and see where Navin had bought Mickey Cochrane from the A's for $100,000 and made him manager of the Detroit team."

H.G. Salsinger of the *Detroit News* had a different version of the story. It goes this way: Navin was still considering Ruth as a possible manager. One morning at 3 o'clock, (yes, three in the morning) Navin's phone rings and a sleepy Navin answers.

"Hello, this is Babe Ruth. I'm calling from San Francisco ... to find out if you want me as manager. I'm leaving for Hawaii and I want an answer right now—yes or no."

Navin, irritated at being awakened at three in the morning and even more irritated at Ruth's brusque ultimatum, answered:

"Since you put it that way, the answer is 'no'!"

Salsinger claims that Ruth just missed two other managerial jobs, maybe three. Larry MacPhail was the boss at Cinci and wanted the Babe as his manager, but at the time could not get him waived out of the American League.

Then there was the Boston Red Sox team, the team that had brought Ruth to the big leagues as a pitcher. Boston owner Tom Yawkey had promised Ruth that when he made a change in managers Babe would have the job. The promise came in late 1934.

Ruth left for a leisurely trip to the Orient, and here's the way he told the story to Salsinger: "I was lolling in a deck chair when a steward brought me the ship's paper. I started to read and nearly fell off my chair when I came to an item saying Joe Cronin had got the job of managing the Red Sox. We took a long trip, Europe and everything. When we got back, the second day home, the buzzer sounds and it's Tom Yawkey calling on us. He comes up to see me. I say: 'Tom, you give me a terrible double-cross. You promised me that job and you give it to Cronin.'

"He says to me: 'Well, Babe you know there's things over which I got no control. I wanted you for my manager, but I got blocked out and couldn't do it.' That's the deal I got from my pal, Tom."

In early 1935, all American League clubs waived on the Babe and he joined the Boston Braves as a player and vice president. He was under the impression that he would be made manager at the end of the season, replacing Bill McKechnie. Ruth appeared in 28 games and had 13 hits—6 of them home runs. The club seemed in no hurry to fire McKechnie and make Ruth the manager. He also discovered that the vice president job was just an empty title. Ruth had a batting average of .181 when he was released on June 2.

In 1938 Larry MacPhail, by then general manager of the Dodgers, signed Ruth as a coach. But it was an unhappy venture for the Babe. He was released near the end of the season, and that severed his final connection with the major leagues. He never became a manager. He almost made it, but it just didn't work out for baseball's super, super star.

It's hard to believe that Casey Stengel has been dead since 1975. It seems that Casey is still with us. Almost every day in baseball I hear somebody recall an incident about him or remember something that he said.

He was a flake and a joke and a clown; but when he took over the Yankees in 1949, he showed people that he could manage. He won five pennants and five World Series in his first five years. And in his 12-year tenure, he captured 10 pennants and seven World Series.

The Yankees told Casey he was too old and dumped him. He went across town to the impossible Mets and was able to make even them competitive.

I think Casey will be more remembered for his personality than for his playing—or even his managing. He was baseball's best ambassador. He knew how to use the media, especially the writers who traveled with his clubs. And he was great with the fans. Not all his players appreciated him as much as the writers and fans: To some of them, his tongue was too sharp and his wit was too sarcastic. However, none of those players ever complained about the World Series checks that Casey helped them cash.

If you sat with Stengel in his dugout before a game, he would answer your questions, but sooner or later he would be asking you about various players you'd seen, or about players on the Tigers. That was one of the ways he gathered information for that fertile brain of his.

Players with bad tempers have been legendary in baseball ... Wes Ferrell, Lefty Grove, Billy Martin, Kirk Gibson, just to name a few. Those guys had volcanoes inside—and now and then they had to erupt.

But the temper that led the major leagues had to belong to a man who once managed the Tigers—Fred Hutchinson. Normally a lovable bear sort of a guy, Hutch could explode like no other. Broken chairs and busted lights in stadiums testified to that. He was explosive, but his players (though they feared his terrible temper) had a deep-abiding love for Hutch.

Hutchinson was a pitching sensation in the minors. In the 1938 season he won 25 games for the Seattle team, then in the Pacific Coast League. The Tigers paid big money for Fred and he pitched for them from 1939 through 1953. His best Tiger year was 1947, when he won 18 and lost 10. In July of 1952 he was named Tiger manager. He held that job through the '54 season. Later he managed the Cardinals and the Cincinnati Reds. Fred's only pennant winner was the 1961 Reds team, which lost to the great Yankee team in the World Series. After Hutch died of cancer in 1964, the Reds retired his uniform—number "1."

There are many stories about Hutch's temper, but one that symbolized how competitive he was happened one afternoon at the Polo Grounds in New York. The Reds were playing a double-header against the Mets. In those days Cincinnati was a good, solid team. The Mets were a joke and very seldom won a game. But this time the Mets beat the Reds in both games.

At the Polo Grounds, both clubhouses were above the bleachers, past deep center field, a long walk from the dugouts. After the second game the players emptied from both benches and were making that long walk. But the Cincinnati bench was not totally empty. There sat Fred Hutchinson, all by himself; and he was steaming. He'd smoke a cigarette, then stomp on it; but even then you could still see the smoke.

After a half hour of sitting, Fred got up and went to the dugout phone. He dialed the Reds' clubhouse and told the clubhouse man, "If there's any of those so-and-sos still there, tell 'em to get out ... I'm coming in."

The clubhouse man said later that when the phone rang there were 13 to 15 half-dressed players around. But when Hutchinson walked in three minutes later, there was nobody there but that one clubhouse man. They knew about Hutch's temper and they didn't want to be around to bear the brunt of it. He was a tough loser, Fred Hutchinson, but quite a manager.

When Sparky Anderson took over as manager of the Detroit Tigers in mid-season of 1979, he became the 15th big-league manager I had worked with as a broadcaster.

My first one was the late Burt Shotton at Brooklyn. Burt will not go down in baseball history as a managerial giant, but he has always meant something special to me because he was the first.

Shotton didn't really want to manage at that time, the summer of 1948. But Leo Durocher had left Brooklyn to jump across the river and manage the Giants. So, Branch Rickey phoned his old pal Burt and begged him to take over the Dodgers—again. Shotton—who had managed in Philadelphia in the late '20s and early '30s—didn't really want to leave those productive fishing holes around his hometown of Bartow, Florida, but he did it for his old crony Branch.

Burt had won the pennant for the Dodgers in 1947. That was the year he replaced Durocher for the full season when Leo had been suspended by commissioner Happy Chandler. In '48 the Dodgers finished third under Leo and Shotton. But in '49 the Brooks, under old Burt once more, swept to a pennant. Shotton stayed one more year, finishing in second place in 1950. He was succeeded by Chuck Dressen.

Shotton was low-keyed. If the Dodgers won or lost, you could hardly discern the difference in Burt's manner. He never put on the uniform. He managed from the bench, dressed in a pair of slacks and a Dodger warm-up jacket. But he had the players. And he was a winner.

In '48 I came up in August to broadcast for the Dodgers, and I lived at the Bossert Hotel in Brooklyn Heights. It was sort of a casual company barracks for the Dodgers. Shotton lived there, too. So did Hugh Casey, the big relief ace.

These two allowed me to ride to the park and back with them every day. What a thrill for me! Casey was a big, blustery cigar smoker. Shotton was a bespectacled gray-haired grandfather. But together they loved to talk baseball, and I certainly enjoyed listening.

Both were admirers of Branch Rickey. Casey used to say, "I hear a lot of talk about Mr. Rickey being cheap. He's not cheap. He's just a good businessman. He'll try to get you to sign for a shotgun or a bird dog, but you've got to hold your ground."

Shotton and Rickey's friendship went all the way back to their playing days. "He's the greatest," Burt used to say about the Brooklyn boss. "He's so far ahead of anybody else in baseball that it's not even close."

The press had mixed feelings about Shotton. Some reporters felt that Rickey had taken friendship too far in hiring him. Others respected his ability. He was quiet, but he was accessible. Yet, he was a reluctant big-league manager. "Kindly ol' Burt," as Dick Young used to call him, would have preferred fishing in Bartow, Florida to managing the big-league Dodgers. But he was there, doing the job for his old pal, Branch Rickey. And, besides, he was my first manager.

Since I arrived in Detroit in 1960 to broadcast the Tiger games over WJR, the team has used 12 managers. Let's thumb through the list and nail down what they were like—thumbnail sketches, if you please. In the order of their appearance:

Jimmy Dykes: A stumpy pixie full of gags and good humor. He loved cigars and people—not necessarily in that order. The clubhouse was full of kids and visitors.

He knew he didn't have a good team and was relaxed about it—and about everything else.

Joe Gordon: the man Bill DeWitt acquired when he swapped managers with Cleveland. Joe was another good-humor man, but he didn't seem to enjoy being a manager. He couldn't understand his players not playing better and not getting a kick out of playing the game. When we were flying back from the final game in Kansas City, Joe told his players he was quitting. There was not a single newsman on the plane to break the story.

Bob Scheffing: Gruff on the surface. We called him "Grumpy." Steady manager who was loved by his players. Outstanding storyteller and a warm, friendly man. Almost won a pennant in 1961, then faded fast. I have a special spot for Bob because he was my radio-TV partner after he lost his manager's job.

Charlie Dressen: Feisty and capable. A down-to-earth realist. Some felt Chuck suffered with an enlarged ego ("I"-strain). I simply found him to be honest and forthright. "Hold 'em 'til the eighth and I'll think of something," was his battle cry.

Bob Swift: Managed only a short time in 1965 and 1966. He took over after Dressen died. At that time, Bob himself was dying of cancer and he died at the end of the 1966 season. A quiet, thoughtful, no-nonsense man.

Frank Skaff: Another Tiger manager in that fateful '66. Didn't manage long enough to show his real ability. Insightful and intelligent. He later triumphed over a heart attack.

Mayo Smith: "America's Guest," they used to call him when he toured the pressrooms as a scout and regaled his listeners with baseball tales. As a Tiger manager he was more subdued, but still loved to have a good time. He was conservative as a manager. His switch of center fielder Mickey Stanley to shortstop in the '68 Series was completely out of character for Mayo—a bold gamble that proved to be a stroke of managerial genius.

Billy Martin: The most enigmatic of all managers. A different person every day—almost every hour. Impulsive, brilliant, vindictive and sometimes downright cruel. A streetwise hustler who knew the game but didn't always know himself.

Joe Schultz: Martin's late-season replacement in '73. The epitome of the old baseball school. He'd done it all: batboy, player, coach, manager. Jovial and easygoing. Owned one of the game's best wigs, but seldom wore it.

Ralph Houk: Shackled with poor teams in Detroit. He managed one of the three Tiger teams to lose more than 100 games. A loner who was much more lenient with his players than I had expected. His highly reputed "Iron Major" temper exploded only on rare occasions. I enjoyed his sly sense of humor.

Les Moss: A career baseball man. Quiet and steady. Les seemed intimidated by some of the older, more established players. When he got his only real big-league managing shot, he had to be sacrificed so the Tigers could hire Sparky Anderson.

Sparky Anderson: The Tigers' best all-around manager. Knows when to stroke a player or when to chastise him. Great buffer between his players and the media. Always available, always accommodating. The present team is his team. He has put together pieces of the puzzles. Smart enough to build a great coaching staff to help him. An honest man and an outstanding human being.

Here's why big-league managers go crazy. When Al Lopez was managing the White Sox in the late '50s, his team was playing a night game in Baltimore. The curfew for this particular night stated that the game was to be ended at 10:15 to allow Chicago to catch a train to New York.

With only a few minutes left before curfew time, the Sox were leading, 4–3. Lopez had his knuckle-ball pitcher, Paul LaPalme, on the mound, and Dick Williams was at bat for Baltimore. So Lopez walked to the mound to tell LaPalme to waste a few pitches and let the clock run out. As soon as Lopez had returned to the dugout, LaPalme grooved a pitch to Williams. Dick swung and hit the ball into the left-field seats, tying the score, 4–4. As Williams crossed the plate, the umpire suspended the game. The Sox had to return to Baltimore to resume the game at a later date. And when they came back, they lost it—all because Mr. LaPalme didn't waste a few pitches or just hold the ball a few seconds longer.

Jimmy Dykes always had a sly device to emphasize his critical remarks about the umpire's eyesight. He would fill out the lineup card in very light pencil. The umpire would say, "I can't read this." And Dykes would say, "Well, I was telling you all the time that you couldn't see."

Only one manager has led two teams to last place in the same year—John McGraw. In 1902, McGraw started the year as skipper of the Baltimore Orioles. Midway in the season, he jumped to the Giants. Under his leadership, the Giants finished dead last in the National League while the Orioles ended up last in the American League.

In 1910 and 1913, the Philadelphia Athletics played in 10 World Series games. Connie Mack, their manager, made no substitutions—no relievers, no pinch hitters whatsoever—as Philadelphia won each Series in five games.

Bill Armour, the Tiger manager in 1905–06, checked with his wife before he made any pitching selections. If he changed pitchers during a game, he would go to his wife's seat and consult her.

One day the Tiger's Gee Walker was picked off base, killing a rally. Player/manager Mickey Cochrane told the players it would cost the next man picked off $50. The next man picked off? Mickey Cochrane.

Joe McCarthy had some opinions on the secret of managing: 1) You need memory and patience; and 2) You need to know who to keep and who to get rid of. Casey Stengel had another theory: "One-third of my team loves me; one-third hates me; and the other third is undecided." Casey added, "The idea is to keep the third that hates me away from the third that's undecided."

Harry Wright, the Cincinnati manager, in the old days was also a center fielder and had to wear his uniform while playing in the field. Baseball remains the only sport in which the manager or coach dresses like a player.

When Ed Barrow, one-time Tiger manager, was at Boston in 1918 as the general manager, he began the practice of letting customers keep foul balls. Barrow is also the man who converted Ruth to the outfield; developed Honus Wagner at Patterson, New Jersey and sold him to the majors; once hired John L. Sullivan and Jim

Corbett to umpire in a game; and had some great years as the general manager of the New York Yankees.

Rogers Hornsby, when he managed, allowed no food or soft drinks in the clubhouse, yet he allowed a pinball machine and gambled on it with his players.

Cap Anson's wife was the official scorer of the games in which Anson managed. And, at the turn of the century, when Frank Selee was manager of the Cubs, his official scorer was Mrs. Frank Selee.

In 1899, Ned Hanlon was president of the Baltimore Orioles and manager of the Brooklyn team in the same league.

Groucho Marx, manager of the comic baseball team, told the first batter, Jack Benny, "Get up there and hit a home run." Benny struck out. Groucho glared at him and said, "If you are not going to do what I tell you, what's the use of my being manager?"

FOURTEEN

Calling Them as They See Them

"It ain't nothin' till I call it."

Bill Klem

There was an American League umpire named Joe Rue who worked in the league from 1938 through the 1947 season. And like most umps Mr. Rue had to call on the right word at the right time once in a while to get himself out of a tight spot. Of course most of those tight spots concerned a player arguing with Rue over a decision he had made. But there were times, too, when he had to listen to (and take care of) the plain old baseball fan.

One afternoon Joe was working behind the plate and a fan in a nearby box heckled him on almost every decision. One of the teams made a substitution and Rue had to walk over near the box seats to make the announcement.

The heckler stood up and yelled at Joe: "Who's the umpire?"

Rue looked daggers right through the fan and answered: "You are, buddy, but I'm the one who's getting paid for it."

Ever hear the story about the ballplayer who was ejected from a game because of something he had done the winter before? It involves our old friend Herman "Germany" Schaefer, who played second base on the Tigers' pennant-winning teams in 1907, '08 and '09.

Germany lived in Chicago in the winter and hung around an old tavern there, the Log Cabin Inn, with a lot of ballplayers, jockeys, prize fighters and umpires. One of the latter was Jack Sheridan, who umpired in the American League in the summer and was in the undertaking business in the off-season. Ol' Jack called 'em in the summer and buried 'em in the winter.

Sheridan had another winter pastime—drinking. One winter night in Chicago, Germany Schaefer came by the Log Cabin Inn and found his old umpiring pal Jack Sheridan fast asleep there. Jack had leaned his chair up against a drain pipe in the kitchen and was sleeping off a few extra whiskeys.

Schaefer climbed to the roof of the place and found the other end of the pipe. He shouted down into the sleeping umpire's ear: "Jack Sheridan, your time has came."

Sheridan got right out of his chair and headed for the bar. He downed a couple of quick shots and tried to figure out whether it was a voice of warning or something he'd eaten.

In a little while he was back in his chair, asleep again. And Germany Schaefer climbed to the roof and yelled into the pipe: "Jack Sheridan, your time has came."

This time Sheridan leaped out of the chair, headed straight out of the door and didn't come back to the Log Cabin all winter.

But the end of the story doesn't arrive until a hot

August afternoon at Bennett Park in Detroit. Only 300 fans watched the Tigers play like a committee: They were losing bad, but no one seemed to care. Jack Sheridan was umpiring back of the plate. And Schaefer was at bat.

The pitcher delivered a pitch two feet wide of the plate. "Strike two," says Sheridan.

Schaefer never turned to make a protest. But for the third time in his life, Jack Sheridan heard that terrible warning: "Jack Sheridan, your time has came."

All of a sudden the small crowd was amazed. Sheridan swung at Schaefer and missed. He kicked at him and missed.

"You're out of the game, you so-and-so," he yelled. And then he chased Schaefer all the way to the clubhouse. Germany was out of the game, chased for his antics of the winter before plus that summertime reminder to Mr. Jack Sheridan.

Sipping orange juice shouldn't get anybody into trouble. Yet, that healthy habit proved most unhealthy for Bobby Bragan when he was managing Pittsburgh in the mid-'50s. Bobby had been ejected from a game by umpire Stan Landes. He returned to the field sipping orange juice through a straw. For Landes that was the last straw. Bragan was again tossed off the field, handed a suspension and a fine of $100. Two days later the Pittsburgh Pirates fired Bragan.

One of the most unusual of all fines happened to a Depression-era pitcher named Jim Walkup of the St. Louis Browns. Jim's manager, Rogers Hornsby, had a strict rule: "Never throw a strike to a batter when you have a two-strike, no-ball count on him. Always waste that pitch." Violation of the rule meant a $50 fine for the pitcher.

One afternoon Walkup had two strikes on Yankee batter Lefty Gomez. He tried to throw outside, but the ball broke over the plate. "Strike three, you're out," shouted the umpire.

Instead of rejoicing that he had fanned the batter, Walkup charged toward the umpire. "You can't call that a strike. It'll cost me $50. Please, Mr. Ump, change that call to 'ball one.'" Nothing doing: Gomez was out and Mr. Walkup was out of 50 bucks.

At least two major-league rookies have been tossed out of games before they even got into the lineup. One of those rookies was Dick Schofield, father of the present-day Angel shortstop Dick Schofield. Dick (Sr.) was seated in the dugout watching his team, the Cardinals, play the New York Giants in 1953. He was a youngster who had never been to bat in a big-league game—or any game in organized ball. Dick became enraged at an umpire's decision, ranted at him and was promptly ordered to leave the premises.

The other instance happened many years ago—in 1913. Bill Klem was umpiring behind the plate in a hot, tense battle between the Pirates and the Cubs. The Pirates had been heaping abuse on Klem all afternoon. Finally, the ump stepped toward the Pirate dugout and shouted: "One more peep outta' you crybabies and I'll run all of you outta' the park."

It was then that manager Fred Clarke of the Pirates sent a pinch hitter to the plate—it was to be the youngster's debut. He was very nervous as he approached the plate—so nervous he could hardly pronounce his own name.

"C'mon," barked umpire Klem to the kid, "we ain't got all day. What's your name, anyway?"

"Booe," came the hesitant answer.

Klem exploded. "You're outta' the game, you fresh busher. I'll teach you to get smart with me."

Astonished, the rookie backed off in fright. He was bewildered as he returned to the dugout. His name was Everitt Booe.

A Baltimore catcher was once ejected from a game for praying. Ray Murray's prayer was slightly different from the church variety. This one happened at Comiskey Park in Chicago in 1954. Umpire Ed Hurley had just called a 3–2 pitch ball four on a Chicago hitter. Murray turned toward the umpire and kneeled in a prayerful attitude, saying:

"Dear Lord, I know that pitch was a strike. Thirty thousand people in this ballpark know it was a strike. But they have good eyes. Dear Lord, give this poor blind man a pair of good eyes and then he'll know it was a strike."

One year Earl Weaver was managing the Elmira team and having a hot race with Williamsport, managed by Frank Lucchesi. On a close play, the umpires ruled against Elmira. Weaver charged umpire Fred Blandford and began to fume. The other two umps joined in, but they wouldn't change the decision.

Weaver then laid down, face up and motionless on the pitcher's mound. Blandford told him to get up, he was out of the game. Weaver wouldn't move. He looked up and saw Lucchesi, who had gone back to the bench to get a camera. Lucchesi was taking pictures and howling with laughter.

"What about him?" yelled Weaver. "What about him and that camera?"

"Now get on out," said the ump. "Nothing's gonna develop from that, except you're out of the picture."

Fair is fair, and there have been times when umpires have had to pay for wrongdoings—just like players and managers.

I can think of one ump who had to pay twice within a couple of years. The umpire was that great American League arbitrator, Bill McGowan, who some say was the best who ever worked in the American League.

Bill's first suspension came in a game at Washington. During a heated exchange, he threw his whisk broom at a Washington player. For that action, Will Harridge, president of the American League, fined McGowan and suspended him for 10 days.

Two years later, McGowan got another telegram from Mr. Harridge, telling him to send money and take a few days off. This one came about because Bill abused some St. Louis sportswriters. It was a hot day at old Sportsman's Park in St. Louis, the Browns against the Tigers. McGowan was behind the plate and the Tigers kept saying bad things to Satchel Paige, who was pitching for the Browns. Mac couldn't put up with the abuse directed at Satch, so he cleared off the Tiger bench—at least he got rid of the worst offenders.

The St. Louis writers were curious. They called on the phone to McGowan and asked what happened. "Tell 'em, I'll write them a letter," the ump told the caller.

That stung one of the writers when he heard the reply. He yelled down to McGowan, "We didn't know you could write."

The insult rang out in the near-empty ballpark and hit McGowan where it hurt—right in the ego.

He turned his head and looked up toward the press box. Now Mac had a voice like a mummy's curse and it rode on the hot, still air upward toward that press box.

"If any of you dopes could write," he shouted, "you wouldn't be in this stinkin' place—you'd be in New York."

The writers complained to the league president and Harridge promised the press that he would suspend Mr. McGowan for two days.

Yes, even the umpires get hit once in a while.

I've always felt that there are not enough umpires in the Baseball Hall of Fame. Only six have made it: Jocko Conlan, Tom Connolly, Billy Evans, Cal Hubbard, Bill Klem and Al Barlick.

Barlick reached the majors at a very young age—25. He went on to work 27 full seasons in the National League, including seven World Series and seven All-Star Games. Now he is an umpiring consultant for the National League. In my National League broadcasting days, he was a standout. He used a great booming voice to call balls and strikes, and he was always in command of his game.

I found him personable and cooperative. But I think the best tribute to Barlick comes from Tiger manager Sparky Anderson.

Sparky played one year in the majors—with the Phils in 1959. He told me about a double-header in Philadelphia where Barlick was umpiring at first. He made a call in the first game that cost the Phillies a victory and got manager Ed Sawyer steaming. Sawyer was still steaming by the time the second game was scheduled to begin. He refused to come out to home plate and give the lineup to Barlick, who was now the plate umpire. Twice he cussed the umpire. Barlick walked over to the Phillie dugout.

"One more word and you're out of the game," he told Sawyer. Sawyer cussed him again and Barlick tossed him out. As Sawyer made his way to the clubhouse, rookie infielder Sparky Anderson yelled from the dugout, "He's right, Barlick ... that goes for me, too."

Barlick whipped off his mask and strode to the dugout.

Sparky had sneaked down the tunnel, but the umpire followed him. Barlick roared at the rookie Anderson. "Young man, if I ever hear any kind of talk like that out of you again, you'll regret it the rest of your life."

Now, it's Anderson's first time at bat in the game—about the third inning. He takes a pitch, just off the outside corner, thinking it was out of the strike zone. The pitch was marginal. The veteran ump must have been tempted to teach the rookie a lesson. Instead, Barlick called, "Ball three."

Sparky stepped out of the batter's box, asked for time, reached down, picked up some dirt, looked up at Barlick and said, "Mr. Barlick, from now on through the rest of my career, you're going to have my utmost respect."

That's not quite the end of the story. After Sparky became manager of the Reds, Barlick came to him and said, "Sparky, I have a protege named Ed Vargo. Take care of him and see that you help me to make him a good umpire."

After Barlick retired and Vargo had become an umpiring fixture in the National League, Vargo came to Sparky. This time he had a protege named Bruce Froemming. It was the same conversation again—two generations of umpires had followed the great Al Barlick, and Barlick himself had been a protege of the Hall-of-Fame umpire, Bill Klem. Quite a lineage.

The late Pie Traynor was not only one of the great third basemen of baseball history, but one of the game's top gentlemen. Pie never used profanity, and only once in his long career was he ejected from a game by an umpire—Bill Klem.

After the incident, a Pittsburgh sports reporter interviewed Klem.

"Why did you toss Pie out of the game?" he asked the umpire. "I know he didn't cuss you."

"Well," said Mr. Klem. "I had to do it to let him recover from his illness."

"Illness? What illness?" asked the writer.

Here was Klem's answer: "Pie came up to me and in a very polite and firm voice, he said, 'I'm getting sick and tired of your silly decisions.' So I tossed him out. I didn't want him to keep getting sick."

Nick Altrock was a fine American League pitcher who spent his later years coaching for the Washington Senators. He also teamed with Al Schacht to provide baseball comedy for many years.

One afternoon in Washington, Altrock was coaching at first base. The umpire behind the plate was Bill McGowan. McGowan was having a bad day, and his decisions were all going against the Senators.

Late in the game, a Washington batter fouled a ball into the grandstand. McGowan looked over toward the stands and saw the ushers carrying a woman out of the park on a stretcher.

He called out to Altrock in the coach's box.

"Did the foul ball hit that woman?" he asked.

Altrock's answer came back quickly.

"No, Bill," he said. "Your last decision was correct, and that woman was so surprised she fainted."

Cy Rigler was 6 feet, 240 pounds. He umpired for more than 20 years and was notorious for delaying the start of the second game of double-headers by as much as 40 minutes so he could enjoy a huge lunch. Once, between games, he consumed five pig knuckles, five orders of sauerkraut, five boiled potatoes, five ears of corn, three Limburger cheese sandwiches, five bottles of beer and three cups of coffee.

Old Jesse "The Crab" Burkett, one of baseball's great hitters, had a crusty disposition. Once when he came up to pinch-hit, the umpire asked, "Who are you hitting for?" Jesse answered: "None of your business." So the ump turned to the crowd and said, "Burkett, batting for exercise."

A church singer friend of Red Jones arranged for Red, the umpire, to go to church with him and appear with him on the program in a special song. The number? Hymn No. 91, "Open Thine Eyes."

Stubby Overmire, one-time Tiger pitcher, won the first game of a double-header for St. Louis. His wife was arriving later that afternoon. Manager Zack Taylor wouldn't let him leave, telling him to stay on the bench and see the second game.

Stubby was miffed. The other players discussed it, and they told the umpire, Bill Summers, about it. Bill was umpiring third base. In the first inning of the second game, he wheeled around and pointed to Overmire who was brooding and silent. Summers said, "You're out of the game." Overmire got to see his wife that afternoon.

Umpires for many years used a long-handled broom to dust off the plate, but a fellow named McCarthy of the Cubs stepped on the broom coming in to score and was injured badly. The president of the National League, H. C. Pulliam, issued an order requiring that whisk brooms be used rather than the long-handled variety.

Red Ormsby was an American League umpire. He made a bad call that went against the home team. A woman behind the plate said, "If you were my husband, I'd give you poison."

Red Ormsby replied, "Lady, if you were my wife, I'd take it."

FIFTEEN

Spreading the Good Word

"Hell, if the game was half as complicated as some of these writers make out it is, a lot of us boys from the farm would never have been able to make a living at it."

Bucky Walters

This is a very personal story.

One morning as I got up, I knew I was going to have to tell it. Because when I got up, I looked out the window and saw a steady rain. It took me back to 1934 and the first big-league baseball game I ever saw.

I grew up in Atlanta, Georgia. Like most kids I lived and breathed baseball. But we didn't have a big-league team. We had the Crackers in the Southern League and I saw almost every game they played. I even served as batboy for the visiting teams, and once in a while for the Crackers.

Well, along came 1934. I was in high school then. My uncle who lived in Evanston, Illinois, invited me to come to Chicago for the World's Fair and to see a big-league ball game.

Well, the World's Fair appealed to me, but the prospect of seeing the White Sox in action was even more appealing. I saw the World's Fair in a day or two. During those days the Cubs were off and the Sox were out of town. But the Sox were coming home, and my uncle promised me a game.

It was the Yankees vs. the White Sox: the Yankees with Babe Ruth, Lou Gehrig, Red Ruffing—all the great names I'd read about and dreamed about—and the Sox with Ted Lyons, Jimmy Dykes and Luke Appling.

But it was late September 1934, and the September rains were coming. I looked out the window that day of the game, saw the rain, and my heart sank. It was to be my last day in Chicago. The next day I had a train ticket home.

I watched the skies all morning . . . then came the word that the game was rained out.

"That's all right," my uncle told me. "There's another game tomorrow."

The next day, it rained again—again disappointment enveloped me. Now, I knew for sure it'd be a long time before I saw my first big-league game.

But my uncle came through again. "Listen, you'll stay here until you see a game. I don't care if it rains a whole week," he said.

Next day the skies cleared and I was at Comiskey Park early. I saw Lou Gehrig hit two doubles and Babe Ruth make a fine running catch in the last game he ever played at Comiskey Park. And I went home to Atlanta, a happy 16-year-old.

It was raining again when I was ready to do my first big-league broadcast. August 4, 1948 was the date. I'd been brought up from Atlanta to Brooklyn by Branch Rickey, the Dodger owner, to broadcast the Dodger games. Red Barber, the Dodger announcer, had become ill and I was to replace him.

Talk about nervous—wow! I had seen only one big-league game—that one in 1934. I'd never been in a National League park. I knew no one in Brooklyn—much less anyone on the Brooklyn team.

After a morning meeting with Mr. Rickey, I returned to my hotel room to await the night game. It was raining. It rained all day and it rained into the night. The game was postponed. All I wanted to do was to get that first game over with—to get rid of my nervousness.

I had to wait another 24 hours. Finally the rain stopped. I caught the subway to Ebbets Field and broadcast my first major-league game—between the Cubs and the Dodgers. The waiting had been agonizing—as it had been 14 years earlier. But, as we all know, into each life some rain must fall. In the next forty years, there would be much more sunshine than showers.

I learned early in my career—in a game I broadcast in Atlanta—that in baseball broadcasting, just like in the game itself, dreams don't always come true. At least not right away.

The Atlanta Crackers of the Southern Association played Mobile that night. I was in the radio studio in Atlanta, doing a re-creation. The sponsor, Wheaties, had sent their man down from Minneapolis to monitor the broadcast. This was part of a custom with Wheaties. They were sponsoring about 90 different baseball broadcasts all over the country and once a season, their representative would fly to each city and check up on the announcer.

That night I wanted to be at my very best.

"If I do an outstanding job," I told myself, "maybe he'll go back to headquarters, make a good report on me—and then maybe Wheaties will hire me for one of their big-league baseball broadcasts."

I did my best. I did it alone, too. I mean really alone. I broadcast every play, every commercial, every station break. I didn't leave the mike for the entire game.

The game lasted 21 innings. It ended in a 4–4 tie.

All that time, my subconscious mind reminded me that the Wheaties man was out in the studio lobby listening to me, waiting to give me my big chance.

When I stumbled into the lobby, with an aching back and a sore throat, I found the Wheaties man still there ... but he was fast asleep.

When I came to Tiger Stadium Sunday afternoon, June 24, 1962, I was feeling good. In those days, George Kell and I shared both radio and TV. But there was no TV that day, radio only. We'd been broadcasting quite a few double-headers—almost every Sunday, it seemed—but that day we had a single game. I'd be home early, and the family could have a nice, leisurely dinner together.

It didn't happen that way. The game went 22 innings and lasted exactly 7 hours. In the top of the 22nd inning a Yankee rookie outfielder named Jackie Reed hit a two-run homer off Phil Regan and the New Yorkers won the game, 9–7. Reed never again hit a home run in the big leagues—that was his one and only.

Mel Allen and Phil Rizzuto were broadcasting the game for their Yankee network. Phil has always had a habit of leaving games early. He often wants to get away—to beat the traffic or to just get away. This time he took off for Detroit's Metro Airport after the seventh inning. He was very much surprised when he landed in New York, hopped into his car, turned on the radio and heard a weary Mel Allen still broadcasting the game. In fact, the game was not over until after Rizzuto reached his New Jersey home.

The game ran so long that the Tiger Stadium concession stands had to close because of work laws, and the fans had no food for the final few innings. Nevertheless, more than half of the crowd of 35,000 was still around for the final out.

Detroit used 22 players. New York used 21. Thirteen players played the whole game—all 22 innings. Seven of those were Yankees and six were Tigers. Only four Yankees did not see action: Whitey Ford, Luis Arroyo, Roland Sheldon and Ralph Terry—all pitchers. The Tigers who didn't play were also pitchers: Sam Jones, Paul Foytack and Jim Bunning. Al Kaline was on the disabled list with a broken collarbone.

The Yankees took an early lead, scoring seven runs in the first two innings. But the Tigers had two three-run innings—in the first and third. Then Detroit tied the game with one run in the sixth. And from then on, neither team was able to score until Reed's homer in the Yankee 22nd.

New York had 20 hits, the Tigers 19. Rocky Colavito had seven of those Tiger hits—seven in 10 times at bat. When Rocky came to the plate for his 10th time in the 22nd inning, he went through his usual stretching routine. Remember, he used to step out of the batter's box and with both hands push the bat high over his head and take a huge stretch. That's why I called him Rocky Calisthenics. Well, Rocky's at bat in the 22nd inning, and he goes into his stretching routine. From the Yankee dugout comes the strident New York voice of Whitey Ford ...

"Hey, Rocky, it's the 22nd inning—ain't you loose yet?"

Yes, 22 innings, 43 players, seven hours, a Jackie Reed home run—and another late Sunday dinner.

To all of you budding broadcasters out there, here's a piece of advice: Never mention during a broadcast that a baseball game is taking a long time. It only irks people and nobody is really interested that the game is too long.

If it's too long for the listener, he's already tuned out and is not listening anyway. Take it from me, because I learned the hard way.

I enjoy my job. I like to see baseball games, and I'm getting paid for something that I want to do. So, it is not in my nature to complain about the length of a game. But some fans can get the wrong idea about a broadcaster.

On July 23, 1961 the Tigers played a double-header with the Kansas City A's at the old ballpark in Kansas City. I don't remember anything at all about the first game, but I have an idea it was long and drawn out. I do remember the second one. It was one of those crazy, mixed-up, anything-can-happen kind of games. The Tigers finally won it, 17–14. The game set a record for the longest nine-inning game in American League history. It took three hours and 54 minutes to complete.

It was a game I enjoyed. The Tigers won. There was a lot of excitement with all the scoring and the crazy plays. Just before the game was over, a voice on the press-box intercom informed our booth that the game had surpassed the old mark in time consumed for a nine-inning game.

I put that information on the air. Despite my premise that nobody is really interested in the length of a game, I still felt that this was a new record and deserved a mention. That's all I gave it—just a mention and nothing more.

When I returned home to Tiger Stadium, I picked up my mail and found among the other letters a blistering attack against me. It centered around my announcement in Kansas City about the length of the game.

The words don't come back to me now exactly as my correspondent wrote them. But I do remember that they scorched the paper they were written on.

"You no-good so-and-so," was about the way the letter started. "My brothers and I work in a steel mill. We work long and hard hours. We would love to be sitting at the ballpark, watching a big-league game. And we'd never complain. You've got a lot of guts even thinking that you've got a tough job. Brother, you got it easy. Come to the mill with us for just one day—if you can—and we'll show you what real work is. Next time there's a long game, don't bother us with your silly complaints about what tough conditions you work under and how hard you are working.

"You don't know what work is. And you're lucky to have the easiest job in the world."

The letter went on and on, but you get the idea. The fan had taken my simplest statement and read all kinds of meanings into it. The writer didn't sign his name, so I had no chance to write back and tell him my side of the story.

I know you've heard of "On the Road With Charles Kuralt." The famous news correspondent for years has been on the road traveling across the country and talking with interesting people. Maybe you didn't know that Kuralt started on the road, and also on the radio, through baseball.

Several years ago, at a quiet dinner at Hy's in Toronto, Kuralt told me how it happened. Kuralt had always been a sort of father figure for me; so it was a shock when Charles told me that as a youngster he used to listen to me broadcast the Atlanta Cracker games in the 1940s. He was 12 years old at that time and he was an avid Cracker rooter.

The next year, his dad was transferred from Atlanta to Charlotte, North Carolina. He was dropping from AAA baseball to class A and he took it as a personal affront. However, he soon became a Charlotte Hornet fan.

At the age of 13, he entered an essay contest conducted by the *Charlotte News*. He wrote an essay about his devotion to the Hornets, and finished second in the contest. The next year he entered again and again finished second. This time the contest judges decided that such a persistent and talented 14-year-old should be rewarded. His prize was to travel on the bus with the Hornet team to Knoxville and Asheville.

Kuralt was ecstatic. He would be riding with his heroes. Also, he was to write a story on each game.

So, here was this 14-year-old (who had never been away from home before) riding into the night with a bunch of hard-bitten veteran ballplayers. There were a few rookies, too, but even the youngest was five years older than schoolboy Kuralt. Charles would write his game story in the press box, ride the bus to the next town and there file his story at the Western Union office.

His editor, Ray Howell, had told him to tell the Western Union clerk that he wanted to use "Press Rate Collect." Kuralt says that was the thrill of his boyhood—going into a Western Union office, throwing back his shoulders and saying "Press Rate Collect."

The *Charlotte News* printed Kuralt's articles and he became a local celebrity. The radio station called and hired the 14-year-old to do color on the home broadcasts of the Hornet games. He couldn't drive a car, so Charles' dad would drop him at the park, listen to the radio and return for him at the end of the game. That was Charles Kuralt's debut on the radio.

Now, he's a radio and TV star, and one of America's most famous shows is "On the Road With Charles Kuralt." But, remember, he first went on the road and he first went on the radio as a 14-year-old baseball expert with the Charlotte Hornets.

Harry Heilmann died on the eve of the All-Star Game staged at Detroit's Briggs Stadium in 1951.

His death brought a flood of tributes from all over the

country. He was loved and respected by those who had seen him play and also by many who had never seen him in uniform but had listened to his outstanding radio broadcasts of Tiger games.

His broadcasts are legend now. And even though he is in the Baseball Hall of Fame at Cooperstown, New York as an outstanding hitter, he is even better remembered in Michigan for his work on the air. Heilmann began broadcasting Tiger games in 1934 and worked at the mike for 17 years. At first he was on an outstate network. (Ty Tyson was then heard on the Tiger games in Detroit.) Later, Heilmann was on both the local station in Detroit and the entire network. He was a warm, friendly man and these qualities showed through his work on the radio.

He sprinkled his broadcasts with anecdotes from his playing days. In those days, broadcasters didn't travel with their teams, so Heilmann became an expert at re-creating games using only a Western Union ticker, his diamond background and a vivid imagination to make the game come alive for his audience. Often he would perform such a feat before a live audience—in a theatre, store window or hotel lobby.

Heilmann stayed on the air almost to the end. He fought a painful illness, but still he wanted to be part of the baseball scene. Harry Heilmann brought good times to millions of listeners.

Sparky Anderson is a busy man these days, directing the fortunes of his Tiger teams. Sparky is also busy in a lot of other ways. Not many people know it, but he often visits sick youngsters in the local hospitals, he works with charities and very often is speaking at luncheons and banquets.

But speaking at banquets and luncheons goes with the territory. It's part of the job for all of us who are part of the baseball scene. Winter, in particular, means the banquet season: rubber chicken, bullet peas, watery mashed potatoes, and, of course, the after-dinner speaker.

Right now, I'm speaking for the speaker. I know that he sometimes abuses his audience; but he, too, is often abused—as often as the menu.

In New York I used to do a lot of speaking. In Detroit I still do. But in the middle part of my broadcasting career—the six years I spent in Baltimore—I spoke at so many banquets that most folks thought I was never really born, just found on a menu. Somebody burped once on a Baltimore bus and I got up and spoke for 20 minutes.

Something happened to me in Baltimore that is typical of what happens to speakers. A group had called my sponsor, the brewery, to ask me to speak to 800 people. A baseball film would be shown and the meeting was set for 7 p.m. Well, I arrived shortly before 7:00 and found four people in the huge auditorium.

"Maybe they'll start coming in later," said my host.

We waited another 45 minutes. Five more people came in. We were still 791 short of the estimated attendance.

The program began with the showing of the baseball movie. In the middle of the movie, the projector broke. The lights went on. I sat with the nine other people, waiting for someone to repair the projector.

My host—and self-appointed emcee—gave me a glimpse and spoke.

"While we're waiting to get the projector fixed, Ernie Harwell is here and he wants to make a speech."

The only speech I wanted to make at that moment was a big, fat goodbye; but I stuck it out. I spoke for about five minutes and sat down—hoping that the movie would soon start again so our combined embarrassment would be covered by a merciful darkness.

Another of my embarrassing moments came during my second year in Detroit. The late Joe E. Brown, then 70 years old, was emcee at a charity dinner. Joe had been a baseball fan all his life. He had played semi-pro ball and one year he announced the Yankee games on TV.

I was at the dinner to introduce the Tiger players. And here is how the 70-year-old Brown introduced the 43-year-old Harwell:

"Next we'll hear from a fellow that you fans have known here in Detroit for many years. I can remember when I was a youngster living in Toledo, I used to listen to him every day on the Tiger broadcasts."

Joe was 26 years old when I was born. The first baseball broadcast in history didn't occur until he was 29. At that time I was three. Also, I did not broadcast in Detroit until he had reached the age of 69.

The sad part of the whole story is that Joe E. Brown was a fine comedian, but this time he was completely serious. Somehow, he believed what he was saying and he laid it on thick.

Once in Baltimore I was speaking before the Young Men's Chamber of Commerce. During the luncheon, the toastmaster and I had a delightful conversation. He was highly complimentary of my sports broadcasting and very much interested in me. By the time the dishes had been cleared away, I felt he and I were fast friends.

He rose and started his introduction.

"Now, folks," he said "it's our pleasure to hear from a gentleman we all know. In fact, he's one of the best-known men in our city. We hear him almost every day or night on radio and television. His name is always on the tip of every tongue in our city. In fact, we know him so well that we look on him as practically a member of our own household. Here is, is ... "

And then he forgot my name.

He stood there for what must have been 30 seconds, but it seemed like an hour. He simply could not remember my name.

I got up, laughed it off and went on with my speech.

One year in Arizona, the Elks honored the four baseball clubs training in the state. I was on the program as a representative of the Baltimore Orioles.

A friend of mine had called me to say that he was a close friend of the emcee; also, that the emcee needed some information on me, and would I see the emcee before the dinner and tell him some of my background.

Well, I've been a master of ceremonies often. I know how busy one can be just before a banquet. So, I wrote on an index card a few bare facts about myself. I felt that this would save the emcee some time. He would not have to write down anything and yet he would have a basic knowledge of my background.

It was a good plan—until it backfired.

When the emcee introduced me, he said this:

"I don't know what kind of announcer this next speaker is, but I do know that he is quite a publicity man for himself. Here is what he wrote out about himself."

Then he read the facts on the card.

Later, I was telling the episode to a Spanish-speaking friend of mine. When I mentioned the emcee's name, my friend said, "You know that name in Spanish means 'horse-manure.' You should have said to him, 'Thank you very much, Mr. Horse-manure.'"

Sportswriters have always been heroes of mine. My start in baseball was as a writer. And I probably would never have been in radio, except that when I graduated from college I couldn't find a sports-writing job.

I've always felt that we've been very lucky in Detroit. We have two fine papers—very competitive. And the sports writing in both papers is certainly high quality.

But the first big-league writers I knew were in New York. When I broke in with the Brooklyn Dodgers in 1948, some real stars of the sports-writing world were covering that team: Roscoe McGowen of the *Times,* Harold Rosenthal of the *Herald-Tribune,* Joe Reichler of the Associated Press, Milt Richman of United Press International, and Herb Goren of the *Sun* were just a few. The syndicated writers were there, too: Granny Rice, Red Smith, Westbrook Pegler, Frank Graham and others.

I think the first guy I met was Dick Young, and he became one of my New York favorites. Young was streetwise and realistic; no literary airs about him. Yet, he could write as neat a game story as anyone I knew. Later in his career, Dick became an outstanding columnist. Like so many of those guys, his favorite sport was baseball, and he seemed to excel at it.

Some of Dick Young's leads are still quoted when people talk about game coverage. One of my favorites came when I was with the Giants. Dick was still covering the Dodgers at the time. New York and Brooklyn played a day/night double-header (two admissions), something we don't see anymore.

Young started his story this way: "At Ebbets Field today the Dodgers and the Giants played a day/night double-header and that was the difference in the two teams."

What a way to write it.

Once when the Dodgers had routed the Giants in another game, this time 21–6, Young began his report this way: "This story belongs on page 3—with the rest of the ax murders."

Remember that old Longines' commercial: "The world's most-honored watch"? Well, Dick Young wrote a lead that parodied that ad. When 6'8" pitcher Gene Conley of Milwaukee made an error and lost the game, he wrote, "Long Gene made the world's most honored botch." Wow!

After the Dodgers left Brooklyn, Dick Young switched to the Mets. When they finally won their first division victory in 1969, he wrote: "In the most momentous accident since Columbus set out for India, the Amazin' Mets clinch the National League East. The rest will be easy."

Yet, Dick Young never got credit for one of his best leads of all. It happened in the 1956 World Series. Don Larsen, known as a man about town, had pitched his perfect game. Another writer for the *Daily News* struggled with a way to begin the story.

Young leaned over to him and said quietly: "How about, 'The imperfect man pitched the perfect game yesterday.'"

Dick Young's gone now. He died in September 1987. But I'll always remember him as the top baseball writer in New York.

When the World Series of 1989 was delayed by the San Francisco earthquake, it was mentioned in the newsprints and the rest of the media that this delay was the longest in World Series history. The previous record had been set by the World Series of 1911. In that Series, between the New York Giants and the Philadelphia Athletics, the delays had been caused by a week-long rain.

What those stories didn't tell us was how one of the games during that delay might have been played—except for a nosy sportswriter. A writer named Hugh Fullerton actually postponed one of those World Series games.

Since Philadelphia and New York were only an hour and a half apart by train, there was a lot of commuting between the two cities during the Series. The fourth game was set for Philadelphia and Fullerton was still in New York. Rain had stopped in New York and Hugh wondered about the weather in Philly.

He had an important dinner date that evening in New York and didn't want to make the trip down the road unless it was necessary. They were playing day games in those days, so Hughie knew he'd have to catch the 11 a.m. train at the very latest.

Fullerton grabbed a cab and headed for the train station. But on the way, he came up with an idea.

"Ban Johnson," he said to himself. "That's the answer. If Ban's gone to Philly, the game is being played and my date's ruined."

So, Fullerton directed the cab driver to turn around and head for the hotel where Ban Johnson, the American League president, had his headquarters. Fullerton went to Johnson's room, but found it empty. Weary and resigned to have to go to Philly, Fullerton was on his way out of the room when the phone rang. He answered it. On the line was Robby McCoy, Johnson's personal secretary, calling from Philadelphia.

"Mr. Johnson," McCoy said, "it's not raining here in Philly. But the grounds are very wet. What shall I do? Do you think I ought to postpone the game or not?"

That was Fullerton's opportunity. He was equal to the chance. Deepening his voice to the booming tones of Ban Johnson, Hugh growled into the phone, "Call it off, Robby ... call it off."

He hung up quickly, smiling with an air of satisfaction. He was highly pleased with himself. As he stepped out of the room, he bumped squarely into Ban Johnson.

"There'll be no game today, Ban," he told the American League president. "I just called it off."

"You just what?" shouted Johnson.

Fullerton went on to explain about the telephone call from Robby McCoy in Philadelphia. He omitted his personal interest in postponing the game because of his New York dinner date. As Hugh related the story, a big grin spread over Ban Johnson's face.

"For once, Hughie," said Johnson, "you showed good judgment. Besides, I wanted to stay in New York tonight. I have a dinner date I very much want to keep."

"Yeah," said Fullerton, "I know how that is."

Russell Hamm was an outstanding news photographer in Chicago in the 1920s. One afternoon Russ was covering a White Sox game. Art Shires (who called himself Art "the Great" Shires) was clowning around first base while Hamm was trying to snap a picture. Shires had a full jaw of Peachy Scrap chewing tobacco and was spitting in all directions. He deposited a big blob of tobacco juice all over Hamm's new white shirt. Hamm was mad, but kept his tongue. He didn't fight back. He wanted to, but he had a better idea.

Sitting in the stands behind first base was George Trafton, a big strong man who played football for the Chicago Bears. Both Trafton and Shires had been making noises about becoming professional boxers. So, photographer Hamm went over to talk to football player Trafton.

"You see that big galoot out there at first base?" Hamm said. "He says he can beat you up any time and he'd like to try it."

Trafton took the bait and told Hamm he could take Shires in one round.

So, Hamm went back to Shires and relayed Trafton's

sentiments. Shires waved his arms around and said, "I'll kill him."

It all got back to the press box, this feud. Finally, a Chicago fight promoter, Jim Mullen, set up the bout. He pumped up the match with a flurry of ballyhoo and publicity, and the two Chicago athletes—one from the Bears, the other from the White Sox—met in the boxing ring. It happened the night of December 16, 1929.

Five thousand curious fans jammed into White City Arena. It was a sellout and interest was nationwide.

Today it would be like Cecil Fielder boxing Barry Sanders, or maybe Bill Laimbeer against Bob Probert. People were curious about how these two athletes would do against each other.

But the match turned out to be a flop. Both men were out of shape. They started with a flurry of blows, but soon they became arm weary. They hid from each other the remainder of the five-round bout. The sportswriters called it The Joke of the Century. Trafton, the Chicago Bear, won a lackadaisical decision.

Russ Hamm, the photographer, who instigated the fight, never told anybody that he was the true matchmaker—not until many, many years later. He got nothing out of it, really—only the satisfaction of knowing that Shires, the man who spit on him, took a beating from George Trafton.

At least Hamm was smart enough to let somebody else do his fighting for him. And, in the long run, Art "the Great" Shires learned his lesson: Don't go around spitting on a news photographer.

The famous Casey, who became a part of Americana by striking out, might have fanned the air in obscurity, except for a novelist with a pair of scissors and an actor with a fine sense of comedy.

In those days poems were spotted through the daily newspapers like liver pill advertisements. And "Casey at the Bat," appearing in the *San Francisco Examiner* of June 3, 1888, was just another series of verses from an unknown contributor.

Yet, it caught the eye of Archibald C. Gunter, an American novelist. He clipped the poem, stuck it into his wallet, and forgot it.

A year later Gunter remembered the poem and suggested that his friend De Wolf Hopper recite it at a special Baseball Night showing of Hopper's "Prince Methusalem." Since members of the New York and Chicago teams were to be guests at Wallack's Theatre in New York that evening, Hopper agreed. He committed the poem to memory in less than an hour and inserted it into the second act of the musical comedy. Through it his audience sat spellbound and after the poem's splendid denouement, broke into wild applause. Hopper immediately sensed that Gunter's clipping was more than just another newspaper filler.

From then until he died, Hopper rendered "Casey at the Bat" almost every night, wherever he went. Casey, in fact, overshadowed his entire career, establishing Hopper not so much as the comic-opera star as "the man who made 'Casey at the Bat' famous."

The actor did not know who wrote the epic until 1893, five years after it had been printed. The clipping had been signed "E.L.T." and many claimants to its authorship had thrust themselves on Hopper—some even threatening him with lawsuits. But he was unconvinced until one night in Worcester, Massachusetts. That evening he received a note backstage that the author of "Casey at the Bat" would like to meet him. Stepping from his dressing room, Hopper confronted a rather mild-mannered young man, handsomely dressed and reflecting a high station. He was Ernest L. Thayer, son of a Worcester manufacturer.

He told Hopper his story. Yes, he had written "Casey at the Bat" in San Francisco after going to the coast from Harvard with his classmate, William R. Hearst. He was pleased that Hopper had brought fame to the poem.

As to who was the Casey which the poem portrayed, Thayer gave no hints. Many since then have claimed to be the inspiration for the verses, but Thayer never singled out any model for his Mudville slugger.

There is no doubt that "Casey at the Bat" has established itself as one of America's most popular ballads. "The poem is unique," Hopper once said. "It not only is funny and ironic, but also excitingly dramatic, with the suspense built up to a perfect climax."

Ernest L. Thayer wrote it and De Wolf Hopper made it famous; but if Archibald Gunter had not clipped the poem from a newspaper, Casey never would have become baseball's classic strikeout victim.

A wave of laughter once swept through the stands in Washington at old Griffiths Stadium when the P.A. announcer said, "Before the game is resumed, spectators in front row boxes must remove their garments." After an embarrassed pause, he added, "Coats must be removed from the railings."

Players were gabbing about old age creeping up on them. One said it first shows in your eyes. Another said you notice it first in your legs. The third one said, "Nope, you first notice it in your write-ups."

In 1885–86, the Reds had a manager who was also a sportswriter—O.P. Caylor. The team dropped from second to fifth place.

When Ben Chapman managed the Phillies in the late '40s, he explained why he listened to the radio: "When I can't make up my mind about changing a pitcher or putting in a pinch-hitter, I listen for ideas the announcer has ... then I do the opposite."